The World at War

This edition published 2023
by Living Book Press
Copyright © Living Book Press, 2023

ISBN: 978-1-76153-006-7 (hardcover)
        978-1-76153-007-4 (softcover)

First published in 1929.

All rights reserved. No part of this publication may be reproduced, stored in a retrieval system, or transmitted in any other form or means – electronic, mechanical, photocopying, recording or otherwise, without the prior permission of the copyright owner and the publisher or as provided by Australian law.

A catalogue record for this book is available from the National Library of Australia

The Story of
The World at War

by

M. B. SYNGE

EUROPE
BEFORE
THE WAR
English Miles
0
100
200
300
ORKNEY IS
SCAPA
SCOTLAND
IRELAND
DUBLIN
NORTH
SEA
JUTLAND
ENGLAND
WALES
LONDON
DOVER
HELIGOLAND
HOLLAND
ENGLISH CHANNEL
CALAIS
BELGIUM
BRUSSELS
G
PARIS
BAY OF
BISCAY
FRANCE
BERNE
SWITZERLAN
LISBON
PORTUGAL
MADRID
SPAIN
CORSICA
SARDINIA
BALEARIC
IS
GIBRALTAR
MEDITERRANEAN SEA
MOROCCO
ALGERIA

ORWAY
SWEDEN
ST. PETERSBURG
(PETROGRAD)
STOCKHOL
SEA
BALTIC
COPENHAGEN
RUSSIA
BERLIN
WARSAW
ERMANY
GALICIA
PRAGUE
VIENNA
BUDAPEST
AUSTRIA - HUNGARY
RUMANIA
BUCHAREST
BLACK
SEA
BELGRADE
SERAJEVO
SERVIA
ITALY
ADRIATIC
SEA
MONTE
NEGRO
SOFIA
BULGARIA
ALBANIA
TURKEY
CONSTANTIN
-OPLE
ROME
GREECE
ASIA
MINOR
ATHENS
SICILY

Contents

1.	The New German Empire	1
2.	The Kaiser Rules	6
3.	War in South Africa	11
4.	L'oncle de l'Europe	18
5.	The Entente Cordiale	22
6.	The Story of the Balkan States	28
7.	The Years Between	34
8.	The Lull Before the Storm	39
9.	Peace or War	43
10.	The World at War	49
11.	Through Belgium to France	55
12.	Towards Paris	62
13.	A Race to the Sea	67
14.	The Western Front—Ypres	72
15.	The Russian Allies	79
16.	On the High Seas	83
17.	Gallipoli	90
18.	The Western Front—Neuve Chapelle, Loos	97
19.	The Tragedy of Serbia	103
20.	The Fall of Kut	109
21.	The Capture of Bagdad	116
22.	The Western Front—Verdun, Somme	121
23.	The Battle of Jutland	127
24.	Italy Joins the Allies	134
25.	The Last Efforts of Russia	140
26.	The Russian Revolution	146
27.	Germany Loses Her Colonies	154
28.	America Declares War	161

29.	The Western Front- Arras, Ypres, and Cambrai	166
30.	The Dover Patrol and Zeebrugge	174
31.	The Capture of Jerusalem	179
32.	The Conquest of Palestine	184
33.	The Western Front- Germany's Last Effort	189
34.	The Western Front- the Turn of the Tide	197
35.	The Armistice	203
36.	The Peace Treaty	210
37.	A New Europe	219

1. THE NEW GERMAN EMPIRE

"Was ist des Deutschen Vaterland?
Ist's Preussenland? Ist's Schwabenland?
Ist's wo am Rhein die Robe blüht?
Ist's wo am welt die Möve zieht?
O nein! O nein! O nein!
Sein Vaterland musz grösser sein."

—E.M. ARNDT.

As the British Empire grew in size and prosperity during the long reign of Queen Victoria, so the German Empire—united in 1870 after the Franco-German War—entered on a period of triumph and achievement more splendid than anything the world has known in modem times. And it is one of the greatest tragedies in European history that this progress was suddenly arrested with the first shots of the Great War in the summer of 1914.

Look back at that triumphant scene at the Palace of Versailles in 1870 when amid rare enthusiasm William I., King of Prussia, was proclaimed Emperor of a united Germany! At his side stood Count Bismarck, the man who had worked with his royal master for the last eight years, the man to whom the old King owed his throne and now his Empire. Although no longer young, Bismarck was in the full vigour of life. His tall figure, his powerful head, his severe expression made him almost as imposing a figure as William I., who was fifteen years his senior.

Such were the heads of the new Germany, a land which was

to dominate Europe for the next forty-four years and then to fall with a mighty crash.

France had a heavy price to pay to her German conquerors. The indemnity demanded from her was double the sum that the war had cost Germany, and she had to give up besides her rich lands of Alsace and Lorraine with their border strongholds of Strasbourg and Metz.

"France must be so completely crushed, that she can never again come across our path," commented her conquerors.

France was wounded, but not killed. Her thrifty citizens set about their colossal task, patiently bearing the burden of overwhelming taxation. They repaired the havoc of war with amazing rapidity under the veteran President of their new Republic, until, in the space of four years, the great war indemnity was paid off.

Meanwhile the organisation of the new German Empire with her five-and-twenty separate States was no light task. To bring into line four Kings, six Grand Dukes, and many smaller Principalities with all their differing manners and customs, needed the genius of a Bismarck, but with the first meetings of an Imperial Council and Reichstag, he could exclaim with confidence: "The unity of Germany is completed."

For the next twenty years Bismarck was the foremost figure in the politics of Europe.

But it was not the "Iron Chancellor" alone who accomplished such great things for the German Empire. The German people, flushed with victory, had boundless ambition and limitless strength. In industry, population, wealth, and power they went forward with amazing strides. Their success was due to the splendid qualities of the people themselves; with their genius for organisation, they applied themselves to winning triumphs in peace, as they had won victory in war.

Up and down the valley of the Rhine grew huge factories, while forests of chimneys arose as they had done in Central England years before. Lorraine, recently taken from France, supplied an abundance of iron ore, and a great industrial development lay in her huge stores of coal and iron.

German goods soon found their way to all parts of the world. There was outside work to be done too.

The new German Empire must be in close alliance with the neighbouring States of Europe. The world must be at peace—old wounds must be healed, old jealousies annulled.

Alexander III., Tsar of Russia, and Francis Joseph, Emperor of Austria-Hungary, were invited to Berlin as guests of William, the first German Emperor. It was a brilliant affair, this Three Emperors' League, and made for the peace of Europe for some years.

"We must make greater exertions than other Powers," said Bismarck, "on account of our geographical position. We lie in the middle of Europe; we can be attacked from all sides."

Great Britain was not included in the League, and Queen Victoria is reported to have commented: "We are well out of it."

To safeguard his conquests Bismarck set about securing an efficient army to protect the Fatherland, which, as he had remarked, could be "attacked from all sides."

But shadows were falling athwart the newly born Empire.

In 1888 the old Emperor William I. died just before his 91st birthday, and with him passed the support on which Bismarck's power had rested. The short and tragic reign of his son Frederick—already stricken with cancer of the throat—forbade the raising of any points of conflict during his ninety days of sovereignty.

His death made his son, William, the third German Emperor.

On that fateful day in June 1888, the new "Kaiser," aged but thirty, in helmet and crimson cloak, received the homage of some twenty ruling sovereigns who proclaimed the proud young Hohenzollern ruler over fifty million people.

Married to a German Princess, with four sturdy little sons, the new Kaiser was perhaps one of the strangest characters that ever made world-history. Until his father's illness, he had taken little interest in public affairs. Always intensely patriotic, he loved Germany's richly storied past—always intensely industrious, in a nation of hard workers, he was ever one of the hardest and ablest. Matters concerning the German army appealed to him, and he was never weary of asserting that the army was the true basis of his throne: "The soldier and the army, not parliamentary majorities, have welded together the German Empire. My confidence is placed in the army." That he was genuinely anxious for peace was beyond all doubt. "I am determined to keep peace with every one so far as it lies in my power," he told his first parliament (Reichstag).

To this end, within a month of his accession, the young Kaiser left Kiel in his old yacht—the *Hohenzollern*—for Russia, where he impressed on the Tsar his anxiety for the preservation of peace.

It is said that the old Emperor William I. had whispered to his grandson before he died that, whatever happened, he must always keep friends with Russia.

How he lost that friendship, and how the Tsar of all the Russias was the first to declare war on Germany that fateful day in August 1914, is known to every student of modern history.

Returning by Sweden, he greeted King Oscar, and made a good impression on King Christian of Denmark, the Tsar's father-in-law, during a brief visit to Copenhagen.

The following year, 1889, he spent a week in England, where

he was welcomed as a grandson of Queen Victoria. High appointments were exchanged. The Kaiser was appointed honorary Admiral of the British Fleet, in return for which he appointed his grandmother Colonel of a Prussian Regiment, to be called "The Queen of England's Own."

"I regard the British Navy as the most magnificent in the world," he stated with enthusiasm before he sailed home to Berlin to receive a visit from the Emperor Francis Joseph of Austria-Hungary. The tragedies of the House of Austria had already begun, and but a few months before the Crown Prince Rudolf—the Emperor's only child—had killed himself in a country house near Vienna.

Again the Emperors of Germany and Austria-Hungary vowed eternal friendship.

"Both my people and my army hold firmly and faithfully to the alliance concluded between us," cried the young ruler of Germany as he drank the health of his guest. "The army is well aware that, for the preservation of peace, it may be called on to stand by the side of the brave Austro-Hungarian Army and to fight shoulder to shoulder."

Twenty-five years later found the armies of these two men fighting "shoulder to shoulder" against Europe in arms.

A journey to Greece to attend the wedding of his sister Sophia with Constantine, Crown Prince of Greece, was followed by a cruise to Constantinople, a friendly visit to the Sultan of Turkey, and a dramatic journey to Jerusalem. What wonder, then, if twenty-five years later Turkey threw in her lot with Germany in the Great War!

"I believe I have succeeded in ensuring the peace of the world for many years to come," said the youthful ruler of the German Empire at the end of his first year's reign.

2. THE KAISER RULES

"I charge thee, fling away ambition:
By that sin fell the angels."
—SHAKESPEARE(*HENRY VIII.*).

For the first few months the Kaiser worked with his Chancellor—Bismarck—without friction. But it was not long before he realised that the man who had made Prussia supreme in Germany and Germany supreme in Europe, was—in the eyes of the world—the uncrowned King of the new Germany.

"I discovered that my ministers regarded themselves as Bismarck's officials," complained the Kaiser.

Again and again the strong wills of Kaiser and Chancellor carne into collision, and relations between the yet untried ruler and the experienced leader became strained.

Inspired by self-confidence and a firm belief in his own ability to rule, the young Emperor had fiercely asserted: "There is only one master in this country and I am he. I will tolerate no other beside me. Those who will help me, I heartily welcome; those who oppose me, I shall dash to pieces."

In 1890, the crisis came. The two men met to discuss a matter on which they failed to agree. The Kaiser insisted that his will should be obeyed, if not by Bismarck, then by another.

"Then am I to understand, your Majesty," said Bismarck, "that I stand in your way "Yes," was the tragic reply.

This was the end. Count Bismarck at once sent in his resignation and retired from public life. Thus did he fall from his high estate. The event was of world-wide interest. The importance of it was illustrated by a historic picture in 'Punch' called "Dropping the Pilot." The Kaiser stands alone on the deck of the Ship of State sternly looking down the companion-ladder at the pathetic yet dignified figure of his fallen minister leaving for ever the ship he had piloted for forty-three great years!

> "Great Pilot, whom so many storms have tried,
> To see thee quit the helm at last, at last,
> And slow descend that vessel's stately side,
> Whilst yet waves surge and skies are overcast,
> Wakes wandering memories of that mighty past
> Shaped by a guiding hand.
> Strong to direct as strenuous to command,
> When did a great ship on a great sea
> Drop Pilot like to thee?"

A stern Hohenzollern, with tremendous energy, personal charm and dominating will, William II. now set himself to the colossal task of making Germany a world power.

The fever of expansion had already been at work. The rapid growth of the German population during years of prosperity had stimulated large numbers to emigrate, and many had settled abroad under foreign flags.

"A German who can put off his Fatherland like an overcoat is no longer a German for me," Bismarck had exclaimed with wrath.

It seemed as though Germany was too late to secure a "place in the sun." At a time when Great Britain and France were building up their Empires overseas, Germany was but achieving her national unity.

Up to 1884 there was no German flag flying over German colonies, but in the course of the next few years, she shouldered her way into the colonial world, until she had carved out for herself an immense Empire beyond the seas.

One of the Kaiser's first acts was to frame an agreement with Great Britain, whereby Germany should secure possession over those "vast spaces washed by sun," known to history, for a brief period, as German East Africa and German South-West Africa. But when these African colonies were taken from her in the Great War, it was realised that the Germans were no colonists, that they had brought to the hapless African nations not peace, but a sword, not freedom and happiness, but misery, bloodshed, and oppression.

In other directions, too, Germany cast her eyes for fresh lands to conquer. For many a long year she had yearned for the possession of a little scrap of British territory called Heligoland. It was little more than a windswept rock and practically of little value to England. But it was of immense importance to Germany, as it lay at the mouth of the Kiel Canal, connecting the North Sea with the Baltic. In exchange for the island of Zanzibar, Great Britain ceded Heligoland to the triumphant Kaiser.

"Without a battle this beautiful island has passed into my possession," he said at a banquet given on the occasion. "It is with satisfaction that I receive Heligoland into the fringe of Erman islands which skirt the coast of the Fatherland. The island will be a bulwark in the sea, a port for the supply for my warships and a place of refuge and protection in the German ocean against all the enemies who may venture to show themselves upon it."

From this moment, the Kaiser pushed on the cutting of the Kiel Canal with untiring energy. As Crown Prince he had made himself a first-rate naval expert. The German navy still contained many old and obsolete ships. His was the vision of a strong German navy, worthy of the World Empire of his dreams.

"As my grandfather reorganised his army, so I shall reorganise my navy. The ocean is indispensable to the greatness of Germany," he was wont to repeat.

The great Kiel Canal was formally opened in 1895. Each of the Powers of Europe was invited to send a squadron to share in the festivities, and no less than twenty-three ships, assembled from countries including Great Britain, Russia, France, Austria, and Italy, steamed through the canal on that summer evening in June.

It was "perhaps the happiest moment in the reign of William II." when he and his sons on board the *Hohenzollern* looked on the fine array of ships assembled at his invitation.

It could not be overlooked that the French and Russian ships had steamed together into the canal, and that the French ships alone were not illuminated on that fateful night. After the fall of Bismarck, some coolness had arisen between Germany and Russia, with the result that a dual alliance had been arranged between Russia and France, which had been proclaimed but a few months since.

"It is not the friendship of France and Russia that makes me uneasy," the Kaiser had explained, "but the danger to our principle of monarchism through the lifting up of the Republic on a pedestal."

Nevertheless the opening of the Kiel Canal to the "peaceful intercourse of nations" was an event of great importance in the growth of the German navy.

"Ever since our fleet was established," the Kaiser declared later, as he stood on board a British battleship, "we have tried to form our ideas in accordance with yours, and in every way to learn from you. I am not only an admiral of your fleet, but a grandson of your mighty Queen."

This was in the summer.

The new year 1896 had hardly dawned when there was trouble in South Africa. When a clash of German and British interests took place in the Transvaal, the old Boer President, Paul Kruger, had looked to Germany rather than England to stand by him. He had visited Berlin himself. "If a child is ill," he said in his simple way, "it looks round for help. This child begs the Kaiser to help the Boers if they are ever ill. Now the time has come," he asserted when troubles dawned, "to knit ties of the closest friendship between Germany and the South African Republic—ties as between father and child."

The Jameson Raid of 1896 having failed, the Kaiser at once telegraphed congratulations to President Kruger: "I heartily congratulate you," ran the historic telegram, "on the fact that you and your people, without appealing to the aid of friendly Powers, have succeeded by your unaided efforts in restoring peace and preserving the independence of the country against the armed bands which broke into your land."

It is said that the "whole German nation stood behind the telegram."

Be this as it may, a storm of indignation was aroused in Great Britain, and though the Kaiser tried to dismiss the ugly incident as a "lovers' quarrel," England could not forget the indiscretion.

"The raid was folly," observed the English Prime Minister, "but the telegram was even more foolish."

Inability to help the Boers convinced the Kaiser that a larger navy was more than ever necessary. The appointment of Tirpitz as Admiral gave a new zest to ship-building, and the dream of a High Sea Fleet began to be realised. "A new spirit had entered the Admiralty, and a new spirit was soon to dominate the nation."

A Navy League was founded, and in 1898 the raiser uttered those fateful words: "Our future lies on the water."

3. WAR IN SOUTH AFRICA

"This ideal of Imperial Britain—to bring to the peoples of the earth beneath her sway the larger freedom and the higher notice—the world has known none fairer—none more exalted."

—J. A. CRAMB.

The Jameson Raid had deservedly failed, but south Africa was seething with trouble.

For while Cecil Rhodes was planning for British rule from the Zambesi to the Cape, was not Paul Kruger eagerly scheming for a Dutch sovereignty over the same area? He was busy obtaining the best weapons that Europe could supply, and gaining helpful information from German and French experts.

But these larger questions were swallowed up in the lesser, with the demand from the British in the Transvaal for a voice in the Government. This Kruger refused.

"This," he repeated, "is my country; these are my laws. Those who do not like to obey my laws can leave my country."

The British Government, whose leading spirit at this time was Mr Joseph Chamberlain—Colonial Secretary,—now sent out Sir Alfred Milner as High Commissioner to the Cape. The appointment was popular with all parties at home.

A conference at Bloemfontein was called in the summer of 1899, and men strove for a basis of settlement. But the war cloud grew and over-shadowed the land, until one October day the Dutch ultimatum burst upon the world. The two little Boer Republics—the Transvaal and the Orange River Colony—had joined hands and were at war, not only with Great Britain, but with the whole British Empire. The Dominions had been closely watching affairs in South Africa, and realising the justice of our cause they were ready with help should open quarrel arise.

In the spirit of the Australian poet (Hales) Australia, Canada, and New Zealand prepared to take their part.

"Are we only an English market
Held dear for the sake of trade?
Or are we part of the Empire
Close welded by hilt and blade?
If we are to cleave together
As mother and son through life,
Give us our share of the burden,
Let us stand with you in the strife."

Such was the spirit of the hosts that assembled voluntarily at the outbreak of war from all quarters of the Empire, ready to fight, not for the wealth of the Transvaal gold and diamond mines, but for a great ideal.

The Dutch wanted freedom for a single race, their foes wanted equal rights for all white men."

Under the skilful leadership of Piet Joubert, Cronje, De Wet, and others, thousands of swarthy bearded burghers rode to war, well armed, well mounted, knowing every inch of their country, and patriotic to the heart's core. "We will drive the British into the sea," they boasted.

Down into Natal they poured, and on 20th October they took up their position on Talana Hill, not far from Ladysmith, where British forces were collecting. As the mist on the hillside lifted, a curious wailing sound came through the air, and a shell, from a range of some 5,000 yards, buried itself in the soft turf near the British camping ground.

It was the first great surprise of the war, for there was not a gun on the British side which could carry anything like that length. Undaunted, however, they forced their way up the hillside under a storm of bullets and won the summit, but not before officers and men had been mown down by the deadly aim of the foe. Retreating, through torrents of rain, to Ladysmith, some twelve thousand troops were soon besieged under their leader, Sir George White—the Boer army in great force holding the surrounding hills.

Meanwhile Cronje was laying siege to Mafeking, a small town across the western borders of the Transvaal—now famous in history, which was ably and cheerfully defended for 218 days by Col. Baden-Powell, founder of the Boy Scout Association. The day of its relief, 12th May 1900, was one of almost unparalleled enthusiasm throughout the Empire.

> "Just because a little gallant band,
> Eight thousand miles away and very lone,
> With hunger hollowing the fevered cheek
> And parching thirst to grip the throat,
> Against the leaguer's odds have shown
> How the old force of England's fighting creed
> Lives in her sons at need,
> Made soldiers of the fierce baptising flame;
> Because for love of Queen and land,
> Because for honour's sake they played the game,
> Stood to their task from week to lingering week,
> And kept the flag afloat."

Before the end of October, Kimberley, the Diamond City—containing Cecil Rhodes, founder and director of the diamond mines, was blockaded by a formidable force of Boers, not to be relieved till the middle of February 1900.

The whole situation was indeed serious—Ladysmith besieged, Kimberley in a state of blockade, Mafeking closely invested. So far the war had been one long record of disaster with great loss of life, which seemed to culminate in the "Black Week" before Christmas—the most disastrous for British arms during the 19th century.

But even before news of the Black Week had reached England, Lord Roberts of Kandahar, with Lord Kitchener of Khartoum as his Chief of Staff, were on the high seas, bound for the Cape and charged with the management of the whole campaign.

Confidence returned, and early in the New Year the whole situation changed as if by magic.

By 15th February 1900, Kimberley was relieved, by 27th February Cronje and 5,000 men had been skilfully surrounded and captured at Paardeburg, and a week later, dust-covered and weary horsemen made their way into Ladysmith, where the flag had been kept flying for 118 days. The strength of the besieged men was wellnigh spent, their ammunition almost at an end, their food fast failing them—not a day too soon had relief arrived.

Thousands of half-starved men were actually crying for joy. The price of relief was great, for no less than 5,000 of the relieving army had been killed or wounded.

But the dark days were over and the light of the new year was dawning. Lord Roberts now began his great march to Bloemfontein, in the very heart of the Orange River Colony. The Boers had been massing in front of the British troops, but the old British commander swept round their flanks, and avoiding the carefully prepared Boer trenches, he led his army round by the open plains. Then, worn with living on short rations and forced marches under a semi-tropical sun, the army swung into the city "with the aspect of Kentish hop-pickers and the bearing of heroes."

President Kruger had just fled with a handful of followers,

and the Union Jack soon proclaimed that the conquest was complete.

For six weeks Lord Roberts and his army stayed in Bloemfontein preparing for the next move. Enteric fever broke out, and over a thousand men died from the effects of poisoned water.

It was in the early days of May, when the rainy season was past and the veldt was again green, that Lord Roberts was ready for another of those tiger springs that had brought him in the old days from Kabul to Kandahar, from Belmont to Bloemfontein. Once again, with a front of forty miles, the great British army streamed northwards and ever northwards, for the distance from Bloemfontein to Pretoria was over 200 miles. The way was hard, the foe stubborn. Moreover, Kruger, the old President, had promised them a reception at Pretoria that should "stagger humanity."

The capital of the Transvaal was guarded by two hills, and its gateway is a narrow neck between them. On these hills the Boers were posted in strength, and a terrific fire greeted the advance of the British army. But Lord Roberts pushed on; the gateway was bought with a price of seventy men, Botha's army "sullenly retreated," and the treasure-house of Africa was left to the victorious army. Kruger had left Pretoria with a few faithful friends, but refused to leave the country, his old wife being too ill to be moved.

Soon the Union Jack floated from the top of the Raad-Saal, a symbol that the Transvaal as well as the Orange River Colony had been conquered.

Lord Roberts' proclamation annexing the South African Republics in August 1900 was answered by President Kruger in a counter proclamation: "The people of the South African Republics are and remain a free and independent people, and refuse to submit to British rule."

A week later he was persuaded to leave for Europe, and a man-of-war was put at his disposal by the Queen of Holland. Though the Kaiser refused to receive him in Germany, France had shown sympathy with the old man, who died at the Hague before the peace had been signed.

Ten thousand irreconcilables still held the field against the British, and for more than two years carried on a hopeless guerilla warfare. Their astonishing resistance kept the whole force of the Empire busy, till the utmost limits of exhaustion were reached. Not till 20,000 British soldiers had been killed and Boer resistance had worn itself out—not till the spring of 1902—did the leaders dream of peace. It might have been that bitter memories on both sides would have prevented any hope of conciliation. But "statesmanship and good feeling triumphed over fear and revenge."

By the Treaty of Vereeniging, signed on 31st March 1902, the Dutch acknowledged Edward VII. as their king and became British subjects. They were free men, free to return to their homes and rebuild their farms, civil rule would replace the military rule under which they had lived for the past three years, leading to self-government with the other Dominions as soon as possible.

With the surrender of the Boers at Vereeniging, South Africa (apart from the possessions of Germany and Portugal), from Lion's Head to Line, from the southern shores of the Great Lakes to Table Bay, became part of the British Empire.

Two of the most skilful of the Boer leaders— General Botha and General Smuts—soon rose to the head of affairs.

In 1906 self-government was granted, and four years later a still more far-reaching change took place in the Act of Union, from which date a new South Africa came into being. For it represented the "free and unfettered choice" of the people of

South Africa as a whole. The "Great Adventure was undertaken under a stress of deep natural emotion. Men saw visions and dreamed dreams of what the future would bring forth. . . . The slate had been wiped clean, and the new Constitution, written clean and broad and based on absolute equality, was to obliterate the dread past with its misunderstandings and bitter memories and to bring about a spirit of partnership and goodwill."

4. L'ONCLE DE L'EUROPE

"'In the years that shall be I will bind me nation to
nation And shore unto shore,' saith our God."

—STEPHEN PHILLIPS (*MIDNIGHT*, 1900).

No sooner had Lord Roberts issued his proclamation annexing the two Dutch Republics, than he hurried home to England. This was at the end of the year 1900. With his own lips he had been able to tell the Queen the news of his South African success. A few weeks later she lay dying in her sea-girt home at Osborne, in the Isle of Wight.

If the relationship between England and Germany had not always been of the best, it reached its highest point of enthusiasm when the Kaiser hurried across the water to the bedside of his grandmother with signs of affection and distress. There was sympathy in the silent crowds through which he drove with his uncle—then Prince of Wales—from the station, and the words "Thank you, Kaiser," fell on his ears.

Queen Victoria died in his arms, it is said, two days later, 22nd January 1901. The Kaiser's sympathy with the Royal Family produced a deep impression in England. One of the first acts of the new King Edward VII. was to hand his nephew the sword of a Field-Marshal, and to present the Crown Prince of Germany with the Order of the Garter. In the uniform of the Prussian Imperial Dragoons, the new King drove the Kaiser to the station on his departure, 5th February, amid cheering and enthusiastic crowds.

His reception in Germany was of a less cordial nature. Indignant crowds bitterly resented his fortnight's absence in England. For the additions to the British Empire after the South African War were unwelcome to the German advocates of World Power. Not only Germany, but many a European sovereign could claim kinship with the new King of England. Queen Victoria had left thirty-one grandchildren and thirty-seven great-grandchildren, many of whom were married to the Crown Princes and heirs of neighbouring countries. Thus one granddaughter, Sophie, was married to Constantine, the eldest son of the King of Greece; another, Marie, to Ferdinand, Crown Prince of Rumania; another, Maud, afterwards to become Queen of Norway, to a son of the King of Denmark; another, Ena, to King Alphonso of Spain; another, Alexandra, was wife of the Tsar Nicholas of Russia. And it were well to bear in mind these relationships on that day when Europe went forth to war, divided against herself.

The Queen had held aloof from the tangled affairs of Europe. Her interests had mainly lain in domestic and Imperial affairs, and it was natural that her death found England alone in "splendid isolation." It was a storm-tossed country that Edward VII. was called to rule—a country looked on with bitter hatred by those who might have been her neighbours and her friends.

But the youth and training of the new King had prepared him for a more international outlook, and he was anxious to see a better understanding between the larger nations of Europe. How far he succeeded may be gathered from the names that have clung to him after his short reign. He was "L'oncle de l'Europe" and "Edward the Peacemaker."

At the age of thirteen, before France became a Republic, he had been taken to Paris as the guest of Napoleon III. and the Empress Eugenie. Here, even as a young boy, he won golden opinions that endeared him to the French people throughout his life.

"Le petit bonhomme," said the French, "est vraiment charmant."

Forty-seven years later, as King of England, he was to become the "chief architect" of the great Anglo-French Agreement. His relations with Germany had been close and intimate from boyhood, when he first went over to Potsdam, the capital of Prussia, to see his sister Victoria who had married the young Prince Frederick, the Crown Prince.

He had been early to Denmark's capital, Copenhagen—the home of Alexandra, King Christian's daughter, whom he married in 1863, "bride of the heir of the Kings of the Sea." And many a time did he stay with his wife's Danish parents at their castle of Fredensberg, where large family parties were wont to assemble, speaking, it is said, seven different languages! For many a foreign court was related to Denmark, including Russia, Greece, and Norway.

Indeed, Russia was closely connected with both the English King and Queen, for Princess Dagmar, a sister of Queen Alexandra, had married the Tsar Alexander II. On his assassination in 1881 they had hastened to Russia, and been present when the new Tsar Nicholas II. was married to King Edward's niece, Alexandra, daughter of Princess Alice. The King did not live to hear the tragic end of that tragic marriage.

This close kinship with Russia ushered in a period of peace and goodwill with England, and the "entente cordiale" might have extended in this direction, but the Tsar's "intellectual helplessness invited the terrible tragedy which ultimately ended his inglorious career," and the man who signed himself "ever your most loving nephew Nicky," brought his great country to hopeless grief.

King Edward had been to Brussels to see his great-uncle, Leopold I. He had stayed with King Pedro V. of Portugal, whose father, Ferdinand of Saxe-Coburg, was a cousin of both his parents.

He had stayed with Franz Joseph I., Emperor of Austria and King of Hungary, and his beautiful Queen, Elizabeth of Bavaria, at Vienna. He had hunted stag and chamois with their ill-fated only son, the Crown Prince Rudolf, shortly before his tragic suicide in 1889. With Carol, King of Rumania, and "Carmen Sylva," his wife, at their country palace amid the great Carpathian Mountains, he had stayed for bear-hunting, and he knew full well their capital, Bucharest—the "Petit Paris "of the Balkan States.

He knew the first young King of Bulgaria, Alexander of Battenberg, a nephew of the Russian Tsar, and he was both amazed and distressed when he was kidnapped by Russian officers and forced to abdicate. His successor, Prince Ferdinand of Saxe-Coburg-Gotha, was indeed related, though distantly, to King Edward.

Such familiarity with most of the courts of Europe and their rulers was bound to produce good results, and under the King's genial understanding the isolation of England was giving way.

The "petit bonhomme "of 1854 had become "l'oncle de l' Europe "in 1910.

5. THE ENTENTE CORDIALE

"And the soul of the Gaul shall leap to the soul of
the Briton Through all disguises and shows."
—STEPHEN PHILLIPS (*MIDNIGHT*, 1900).

The passing years of growing friendships and better understandings were sure safeguards of the peace so earnestly desired by the King of England. But they were more than this. The "peacemaker of the world" was able, by reason of his personality, to bring nations together on a firmer basis than that of mere personal friendship.

Perhaps nothing illustrates this better than the story of the Entente Cordiale with France.

King Edward had left England in the spring of 1903 for the first foreign tour of his reign. After visits to King Carlos at Lisbon and Victor Emmanuel in Rome, he returned by way of Paris. It was three years since he had visited the French capital. Feelings had run high in France over the South African War, and his reception was somewhat uncertain. Indeed it was hinted that he might be hooted by a people who had warmly received President Kruger on his flight from Pretoria, but a short time since. The King arrived, and the temper of the Parisian populace seemed doubtful.

But he himself dreamed of no danger, and his courage won the day. His first public words won the heart of France: "It is hardly necessary to tell you," he said, "with what sincere pleasure I find myself once more in Paris. The days of hostility between the two countries are, I am sure, happily at an end. There may have been misunderstandings in the past, but that is all happily over and forgotten. The friendship of the two countries is my constant thought, and I count on you all, who enjoy French hospitality in their beautiful city, to aid me to reach this goal."

The people remembered his staunch friendship for them even from boyhood, and cheered enthusiastically. The old wounds of Fashoda and the South African War were healed and all was well again.

A State banquet was followed by military reviews with President Loubet in attendance. French enthusiasm for the King of England grew daily.

When, three months later, the French President returned the royal visit, he was warmly welcomed.

" I hope," said the King with unusual warmth, "that the welcome you have to-day received has convinced you of the true friendship which my country feels for France."

The reply was cordial. "France was the friend of England."

"It is my most ardent wish that the rapprochement between the two countries may be lasting." This was Loubet's farewell message telegraphed to the King.

The sequel to the story is well known.

A General Agreement was drawn up between England and France in 1904 by which the two Governments reached an understanding in all questions under dispute, and further, that France would leave England a free hand in Egypt, and England would allow France a free hand in Morocco.

Now, although this Agreement between England and France was in no way an alliance against Germany, Germany was very vexed with it.

"Everything has been settled and we see that we have been kept systematically aloof," the Germans said bitterly.

With regard to Morocco, "the Farthest West of the Mohammedan world," they were specially concerned.

"France and Spain," argued the Kaiser, "wish to divide up Morocco, which is an independent country under its own Sultan, and close its markets."

Be this as it may, men could not but remember the Kaiser's words at Damascus, but a few years ago: "May the Sultan and the three hundred thousand Mohammedans scattered over the earth be assured that the German Emperor will always be their friend." Suddenly Europe was startled at the news that the Kaiser in his yacht had landed at Tangier, Morocco's capital, and during his short two-hour visit addressed the little German colony there.

"The Empire has great and growing interest in Morocco," he said. "My visit is to show my resolve to do all in my power to safeguard German interests. It is to the Sultan in his capacity of independent sovereign that I pay my visit to-day. I hope that under his sovereignty, a free Morocco will remain open to the peaceful competition of all nations without annexation, on a policy of absolute equality."

Great disquiet followed his lightning visit, feelings ran high, war rumours filled the air, and although peace was maintained, Germany continued to feel aggrieved.

As if to add fuel to the fire, a visit to England by the Prince and Princess of Japan was followed by a new departure from the traditions of British diplomacy, namely, a new alliance with Japan, by which each country pledged itself to assist the other if attacked, and to make war in common.

Meanwhile both England and Germany, though mutually distrusting one another, were seeking new alliances and the forging of new bonds with European countries. Each sought friendship with Russia. The Kaiser was first in the field, and the story of the

"Willy-Nicky" correspondence over a proposed Treaty between Germany, Russia, and France nearly changed the face of Europe.

Both countries were, for the moment, enraged against England, though Kaiser, Tsar, and King were all related to one another and on terms of personal friendship.

"The only way, as you say," wrote the Tsar to the Kaiser, "would be that Germany, Russia, and France should at once unite. This combination has often come into my mind. It will mean peace and rest for the world."

"Best thanks," telegraphed the Kaiser. "Have sent off draft of Treaty you wished for this evening."

A letter followed from the Kaiser: "I at once communicated with the Chancellor and we have secretly drawn up the articles of the Treaty. If you and I stand shoulder to shoulder, France must openly join us. I enclose draft of the Treaty. May it meet with your approval. Nobody knows anything about it, not even my Foreign Office."

The Tsar demurred at certain points, and the Kaiser gave good advice for "keeping the British lion in his den."

"Should the revised draft meet with your approval, it can be signed immediately. God grant that we may have found the right way to hem in the horrors of war and give His blessing to our plans," added the Kaiser.

The Tsar, always uncertain, thought that France should see the Treaty before he signed it.

"It is my firm conviction," returned the Kaiser, "that it would be absolutely dangerous to inform France before we have both signed the Treaty. It is only the knowledge that we are both bound by the Treaty for mutual help that will bring France to press upon England to keep the peace for fear of France's position being jeopardised."

But the months passed on and the Treaty remained unsigned. In July 1905 the Kaiser was yachting in the Gulf of Finland when he proposed a meeting with the Tsar, as "simple tourists and without any ceremony." The monarchs met in their yachts on the shores of the Gulf. The Kaiser at once produced the draft of the Treaty, and persuaded the Tsar to sign it on board the *Hohenzollern*. Then the Kaiser returned home delighted with his work.

But the Tsar was oppressed by his guilty secret."

A letter suggesting difficulties which he foresaw in the future brought a severe reply from Germany. "What is signed, is signed. God is our testator."

France, however, refused to agree, and the Treaty became useless.

Relieved, the Tsar turned for help to Great Britain.

A closer intimacy had been growing between the two countries for some time. This was as acceptable to France, as it was distasteful to Germany.

Since the Kaiser's visit, Russian internal troubles had reached a crisis, and the difficulty of the Tsar in dealing with the growing discontent of his people had become apparent. The story of "Bloody Sunday," 9th January 1905, was never to be forgotten. After oft-repeated petitions to their Tsar, the workmen of Russia decided to act. Led by a priest, Gapon, the peasants of Petrograd, carrying ikons and singing religious songs, marched to the Winter Palace to present a further petition in person to the Tsar.

"Sire," ran the pitiful document, "here are many thousands of us, we come to thee, Sire, to seek for truth and defence. We have been oppressed, we are treated as slaves who must suffer and keep silence. The limit of patience has arrived. Government officials have brought the country to complete destruction. We, working men, have no voice in the expenditure raised from us in taxes. Do not refuse assistance to your people. Destroy the wall between thyself and thy people. Russia is too great for officials alone to rule. National representation is indispensable. If thou wilt not answer our prayer, we shall all die here on this square before thy Palace."

But the Tsar had already left the capital. The troops were ordered to fire on the unarmed workers, with whom were women and children, and some fifteen hundred were killed. It was indeed Bloody Sunday. True, the first Parliament, or Duma, ever held in Russia was held the following year, but it was speedily dissolved, and the discontent was so great that when in the summer of 1908 the King and Queen of England suggested a visit to Russia, the first visit ever paid by an English King, it was deemed prudent to hold the meeting at Reval on the shores of the Finland Gulf. Here they were received by the Tsar Nicholas and Tsarina Alexandra after a separation of seven years. It was a meeting with far-reaching results. For soon the news ran through Europe that the two countries, England and Russia, were in complete agreement "on all points."

In fact, a Triple Entente had been created by England, Russia, and France, as opposed to the Triple Alliance between Germany, Austria, and Italy, which still held good.

"It seems," commented the Kaiser, "it seems they wish to encircle and provoke us."

Be this as it may, he knew that Germany, his Fatherland, stood solidly behind him, and amid universal enthusiasm from his own people the Kaiser went on his way.

6. THE STORY OF THE BALKAN STATES

"That shifting, intractable, and interwoven tangle of conflicting interests, rival peoples, and antagonistic faiths."
—JOHN MORLEY.

But the Triple Entente was not to bring peace to Europe. Only two months after the historic meeting at Reval—October 1908, like a bomb-shell the news spread through Europe that the Emperor Franz Joseph of Austria-Hungary had annexed two of the Balkan States, Bosnia and Herzegovina, with their little mountain capital, Serajevo. Little could men foresee at this time that five years later Austria's heir—the Archduke Francis Ferdinand—would be assassinated here, an event which precipitated that Great World War that was to blaze over Europe for four long years.

Now these far-away Balkan States were the "happy hunting ground" of all the Great Powers, and especially did Austria-Hungary and Russia contend for their friendship.

To the north of Greece they lay, Turkey, Rumania, Bulgaria, Servia, Montenegro, Albania, and the two provinces of Bosnia and Herzegovina, which were just then causing all the trouble.

With its great ranges of mountains, partly bounded by the blue-green Danube, with its sparkling climate and wealth of old monasteries, with its vast plains and moors and lakes, this Balkan Peninsula was a land of mixed races, of constantly changing frontiers, of petty jealousies and short-lived alliances—each

State having its own separate history, each its own independent ruler, each its own interests.

There was consternation throughout the Balkans at Austria's annexations, for, by the Treaty of Berlin, Bosnia and Herzegovina were still part of Turkey's reduced Empire.

For some time past the "Young Turks" had realised that reform in administration was a necessity, and it was never likely to happen under the "Red Sultan," whose murderous record was one of the most terrible in Turkish annals. They had sent an ultimatum to Abdul Hamid, who had been Sultan since 1876, demanding a Parliament within twenty-four hours. The Sultan replied that the idea was excellent, and a Turkish Constitution was at once proclaimed.

On 17th December 1908 the new Parliament was opened at Constantinople amid brilliant sunshine and surrounded by great crowds. Bright scarlet banners with crescent and star in white waved from every window under the domes of St Sophia.

The little Sultan stood there, saluting and nervously clasping his sword. He had suspended the old Constitution which had held for over thirty years!

A strong Turkey might reassert rights over her lost provinces, but Abdul Hamid was weak; further, he was a tyrant, and he must go.

"Down with the Sultan," was the cry.

"Abdul Hamid," ran the proclamation of the young Turks, "who for thirty-three years has exposed the Fatherland to the mercy of infamous scoundrels, who has consented to the deportation of thousands of patriots, who having been pardoned by the nation broke his oath and provoked the destruction of thousands of honest men, is no longer recognised by the nation as its sovereign." Inside his palace the Sultan heard the surrounding troops, but for long he refused to surrender. Then they entered—his thousand courtiers had fled. He was almost alone. "I am a man of ill-luck," he cried. "Go and leave a ship that is sinking."

The old man was exiled to Salonika, and his younger brother, under the name of Mohammed V., reigned in his stead. But Turkey's efforts at reform on European lines were hopeless, and soon the neighbouring States were groaning at her tyranny and cruelty. The Kaiser alone continued her friend.

Indeed, far from being reformed, the condition of Macedonia, left under Turkish rule by the Congress of Berlin, had become well-nigh intolerable, and massacres of the Christians in their midst still continued. Many Bulgarians lived there too under very great hardships.

Now Bulgaria had been an independent country since 1878. The country lay between the Balkan Mountains and the River Danube, and her first ruler had been chosen for her by the Tsar of Russia, who appointed his nephew, Alexander of Battenberg.

"Accept your Prince from me," he had said at the time, "and love him as I love him."

The result was that Bulgaria became practically a Russian province, until the friendship between nephew and uncle gradually cooled and then ended. Alexander was kidnapped by Russian officials in his own palace at Sofia, and hustled out of his kingdom.

After "hawking the vacant throne all over Europe," it was offered in 1887 to Prince Ferdinand of Saxe-Coburg, a man with Austrian and German blood in his veins, then living in Vienna.

He reached the picturesque old capital Tirnovo amid enthusiastic crowds and shouts of "Long live free independent Bulgaria." He advanced to Sofia, the capital, through the terrific heat of midsummer, to be met with—"Welcome, royal Prince. The Bulgarian people thank you for your courage in coming here at this critical moment."

Russia was naturally angry, especially when Ferdinand of Bulgaria married, and his son and heir, Prince Boris, was baptised in the Roman Catholic Church. Later the young Crown Prince was baptised according to the rites of the Orthodox Church, and the Tsar Nicholas acted as godfather.

Russia and Bulgaria then moved forward together, until they separated in the Great War.

To sever the last ties with Turkey, Ferdinand now assumed the old title of "Tsar of Bulgaria," and on 5th October 1908 the principality was converted into a kingdom, by which deed Turkey and Bulgaria were nearly brought to war.

To the North of the Danube from Bulgaria lay Rumania, created in 1861 from several smaller principalities with a capital chosen for her at Bucharest. A few years later the vacant throne was offered to Prince Carol of Hohenzollern, related to the Kaiser. It is said the young Prince had never heard of Rumania, but when the offer reached him he took down an Atlas and finding that a straight line drawn from London to Bombay passed through Rumania, he exclaimed: "That is a country with a future," and at once accepted the crown.

Marrying the beautiful and gifted Elizabeth of Wied, known to the world as "Carmen Sylva," the Prince and Princess soon made themselves one with their adopted country. In 1881 Rumania was proclaimed a kingdom, but the death of their only child, "l'enfant du soleil," made it necessary to appoint an heir to the throne. To this end, the new king's nephew, Prince Ferdinand of Hohenzollern, was invited to come to the court of Rumania, and the succession was settled on him. He married Princess

Marie, granddaughter both to Queen Victoria and the Tsar Alexander of Russia.

A Hohenzollern on the throne and a Hohenzollern heir to the throne, what wonder that King Carol's sympathies were with Germany, or that he could say wholeheartedly: "Although I am King of Rumania, I am and shall always remain a Hohenzollern."

An inland country, with no outlet to the sea, divided from Austria-Hungary by the Danube and from Turkey by a very "chaos of mountain masses," lay Serbia, the most northern of the Balkan States, with its capital at Belgrade.

Soon after Rumania had been declared a kingdom, Prince Milan of Serbia also assumed a royal crown. The newly created king had been on the throne of Serbia since he was a boy of thirteen—a very different ruler to King Carol! To add to his misfortunes, he had made an unfortunate marriage with the beautiful Queen Nathalie. Unhappy and unpopular, he abdicated in 1889 in favour of his only son, Alexander, a boy of thirteen. The country was under a Regent for the next four years, when suddenly, at the age of seventeen, Alexander declared himself of age and took the affairs of his kingdom into his own hands. This threw the country into confusion, which was made infinitely worse, when the young ruler married one, Draga, once lady-in-waiting to his mother, Queen Nathalie. To strengthen his position he now followed Russian guidance in his foreign policy. But, to his Serbian subjects, nothing could justify his unpopular marriage, and the tragic reign reached a tragic end when one June night in 1903, the gates of the royal palace at Belgrade were blown up and the King and Queen of Serbia were assassinated with cruel and savage fury. This ghastly crime sent a thrill of horror through all the countries of Europe.

The regicides at once proclaimed Prince Peter, an exiled

claimant of a rival Serbian dynasty, King of Serbia. The new king was no longer young. He had married Princess Zorka of Montenegro, and lived quietly at Cettinje for some time past with his two little sons George and Alexander. The neighbouring States of Serbia and Montenegro had long been friends.

King Nicholas had been on the throne of Montenegro since 1860. He was an enlightened ruler, and a force to be reckoned with in the Balkan States. His mountainous little land was thinly inhabited, but the Montenegrins were warlike and brave. Not long before his daughter became Queen of Serbia another daughter, Helen, had married the Crown Prince of Italy, Victor Emmanuel, later to become Queen of that country.

7. THE YEARS BETWEEN

"Hate and mistrust are the children of blindness,
Could we but see one another, 'twere well,
Knowledge is sympathy, charity, kindness,
Ignorance only is maker of hell."

—W. WATSON.

Meanwhile with the Balkan tangle growing in the near East, a feeling of distrust and suspicion was apparent throughout Europe. Rumours of coming war were in the air. "The barometer has moved from Rain and Wind to Changeable," remarked the German Chancellor. "Time and patience are needed."

At the same time the German navy grew with a rapidity that seemed out of proportion to her need in times of peace. Just before the dawn of the new century the Hague Conference had met. The invitation had come from Russia.

"It is the desire of His Majesty, the Emperor of all the Russias, that all the nations of Europe might agree to live together like brothers, and to help each other in their mutual needs "ran the call for universal peace by means of limiting the ever-growing armaments. The young Queen of the Netherlands—Wilhelmina—offered her capital The Hague, and in the Palace in the Wood, the first meeting was held and attended by delegates from twenty-five nations, including the United States of America.

In the summer of 1907, the Emperor of all the Russias again invited delegates to a second Peace Conference. Again Queen Wilhelmina offered her capital, and in the "Hall of the

Knights" nearly double the number of delegates attended, and the "Palace in the Wood" could no longer hold them.

In the official language, French, the opening address ran: "Let us not be discouraged from dreaming of the ideal of universal peace and the brotherhood of nations. Let us bravely set to work—our way lighted by the bright stars of universal peace and justice, which we shall never reach, but which will always guide us for the good of mankind."

The Conference again broke down, but it marks an epoch in the history of international relations.

The idea of disarmament grew more and more distasteful to Germany. "We are in the middle of Europe," repeated the German Chancellor, "in the most unfavourable position on the world map. The present situation in Europe is not very comfortable—our fleet is determined by a law solely to defend our coast and our commerce." England became alarmed, and Lord Roberts was not the only Englishman who urged a national army.

"Within a few hours' steaming of our coasts," he pleaded, "there is a people, numbering over sixty millions, our most active rivals in commerce, and the greatest military Power in the world, adding to an overwhelming military strength a naval force which she is resolutely and rapidly increasing." He urged a volunteer army of the nation's young manhood "lest our Empire fall from us and our power pass away." He spoke in vain. Six years later—

> "He passed in the very battle smoke
> Of the war that he had descried,"

and men remembered

> "The weighed and urgent word
> That pleaded in the market-place,
> Pleaded and was not heard."

The same year the First Sea Lord wrote to the King, "That we have eventually to fight Germany is just as sure as anything can be."

King Edward's death in 1910 brought the Kaiser over to his uncle's funeral on friendly terms. The following year the German Imperial Family were received as guests of the new king, George V., with enthusiasm. It seemed as if the "atmosphere was much more genial" and the "old distrust" was passing away. It was but a gleam of hope.

Questions concerning Morocco were again becoming acute. France suddenly occupied Fez, Germany replied by sending a gunboat, the *Panther*, to Agadir. War again loomed on the horizon and again was skilfully averted. Nevertheless the years before the Great World War were full of trouble and unrest.

Among other problems to be reckoned with during the years before the war was Ireland. So absorbing and restless was the state of Ireland in her demand for Home Rule, so many soldiers were stationed there to keep the peace, that Germany felt England was not free enough even to contemplate war. In 1903, when King Edward had visited Ireland, the Home Rule movement was but just beginning.

"Come back, ah, ye will come back," was the cry that pierced through the blaring of the bands and the wild cheers that greeted him in Dublin's narrow streets.

But the King never returned, for the movement directed against Great Britain by a section of her people grew apace during the years of his reign, and at his death Ireland was still in trouble. The Home Rule Bill, by which the country should have her own Parliament and govern her own people, was ready in 1912. But the Northern counties of Ulster did not want Home Rule. Rather did they desire to remain under the King and the

Imperial Parliament. The burning question was discussed far and wide. Could Ireland be politically divided?

Ulster took the matter into her own hands, when half a million Ulster men signed a "Solemn Covenant pledging the signatories to stand by one another in defending for themselves and their children their cherished possession of equal citizenship in the United Kingdom," and used all available means to defeat the Home Rule Bill proposed for Ireland.

Their leader was Sir Edward Carson. Mr Redmond replied for the rest of Ireland that this meant partition of the nation, adding: "To that we Irish Nationalists can never submit."

Then the Ulster men began warlike preparations—openly they drilled, openly they armed for possible conflict.

It was but natural that Ulster's example should be copied. A "citizen" army sprang into being, and a volunteer force gave Mr Redmond a weapon which, it was felt, would enable him to enforce Home Rule.

By 1913 it was pointed out by the extremists in the South, known under the name of "Sinn Fein" (Ourselves alone), that war with Germany was in the air, and that England's difficulty would be "Ireland's opportunity." No one realised better than the Kaiser and his military staff how serious was the situation with which England had to deal in Ireland. Her troops were already massing for possible conflict, and in the eyes of Germany, her hands were too full of home politics to make it likely she would join with France in war.

But Germany was wrong.

The declaration of war welded England and Ireland into one in a common cause. Both North and South pledged their country to the support of the Allies.

"I say to the Government," cried Redmond, "that they may

to-morrow withdraw every one of their troops from Ireland. Ireland will be defended by her armed sons from invasion." Nationalist volunteers and Ulster Covenanters joined the colours side by side. And Irishmen, who for years had been denounced as the sworn foes of England, now gave a new meaning to the words "England's difficulty—Ireland's opportunity." Large numbers made the supreme sacrifice, and their deaths, amid the crash of war, made men ask themselves whether the great historic feud of centuries might not end.

"Then should we, growing in strength and in sweetness,
Fusing to one indivisible soul,
Dazzle the world with a splendid completeness,
Mightily single, immovably whole."

8. THE LULL BEFORE THE STORM

"I have touched the highest point of all my greatness."
—SHAKESPEARE.

While the dispute over Home Rule was apparently absorbing Great Britain, and a possible outbreak of civil war in Ireland might monopolise her fighting strength, a sudden outbreak of trouble in the Balkan States was crippling Turkey—Germany's ally.

The year 1912 opened with dark clouds in the East. The tyranny of Turkey, and her continued oppression of the people in Macedonia, had forced the Balkans into action. A miracle had happened, and the jealous little States were banding together in a League against the common enemy, Turkey.

True, there had been signs of possible union and friendship for some years past. Two years ago, the Tsar Ferdinand of Bulgaria had joined with the Crown Prince Alexander of Serbia and the Crown Prince Constantine of Greece to celebrate the jubilee of King Peter at Cettinje—Montenegro's capital. And in 1912, the coming of age of Crown Prince Boris of Bulgaria had been an occasion for the meeting of neighbouring Crown Princes at Sofia—Bulgaria's capital.

While these social gatherings were proclaimed to the world, secretly the States were arming.

First a Treaty between Bulgaria and Serbia was signed; then another between Bulgaria and Greece—all aimed against Turkey, until in the autumn of 1912 Bulgaria, Serbia, Greece, and

Montenegro had formed a military alliance by which each State was bound to assist the others with all its forces. In the event of dispute the Tsar Nicholas of Russia was to arbitrate.

In August, further Turkish massacres in Macedonia brought matters to a crisis, and the Balkan League burned for action.

In vain the Powers tried to intervene—war was in the air. On 8th October Montenegro precipitated affairs by declaring war, and a few days later, Bulgaria, Greece, and Serbia each presented their ultimatums. Forth to battle went the Kings and their heirs. Overwhelming was their success. Indeed by the end of the month the Balkan States had demolished the Turkish Empire. The old maps of Eastern Europe might be rolled up, for "Turkey in Europe" had ceased to exist. Four small countries, with a population of some ten million souls, had defeated a Power of more than double that number. The plight of the Turks was desperate, and when an armistice was suggested, they only possessed four towns in Europe including Constantinople and Adrianople—not a foot of ground in Europe outside the walls of these four cities!

Again the Powers of Europe intervened to make peace. A Conference was called in London, but difficulties proved insurmountable, and the New Year 1913 had not long dawned when the victors of the Balkan States began to quarrel among themselves over their spoils of war. King Peter of Serbia summed up some of the reasons of the new outbreak when he addressed his troops in July 1913. "The Bulgarians," he said, "our allies of yesterday, with whom we fought side by side, whom as true brothers we helped with our own heart, will not let us take the Macedonian districts that we won at the price of such sacrifices. Bulgaria doubled her territory in our common warfare, and will not let Serbia have land not half her size. Bulgaria is washed by two seas, and grudges Serbia a single port."

The only State that had not joined the League was Rumania. For forty-seven years King Carol had guided the destinies of his young kingdom with wisdom and foresight. At the outbreak of war in the Balkans he firmly believed that Turkey would win, and, with the Germans, was surprised and horrified at her downfall.

When Serbia was thus opening a quarrel against Bulgaria, whose successes offered danger to the smaller States, Rumania joined in. Although King Carol was German in sympathy, although German officers had instructed his army and German engineers had built his railways, yet together with Greece, Serbia, and Montenegro, he feared Bulgarian ascendancy in the Balkans. He knew that Austria would like to enfold Serbia and Rumania in a protectorate, he knew that Serbia again blocked Germany's road to the East, and with the Kaiser's dream of a world Empire the new national spirit aroused in the Balkans might prove fatal to his country's good. The second Balkan War of 1913 was soon over, and an unsatisfactory peace was signed at Bucharest.

"I offer you my most sincere congratulations on the splendid result for which the whole of Europe has to thank your wise and truly statesmanlike policy," wrote the Kaiser to King Carol. "This Rumania must be flattered into submission, and it must be drawn to Germany by every show of friendliness."

Meanwhile the Kaiser was busy at home celebrating the wedding of his only daughter to Duke Ernest of Cumberland, descended from George III. of England, and Berlin was rejoicing at the goodwill displayed on all sides. For among the guests were the Tsar Nicholas on one side and King George on the other. It was also the 25th anniversary of the Kaiser's accession to the throne. This was celebrated by the appearance of a book, 'Germany under William II.,' which was in fact an exhaustive history of the country. "The military machine," it told the people, "was the most perfect in the world; the High Sea Fleet was growing apace; the widening of the Kiel Canal was almost completed; the country was rich; the people well-educated and fully employed; the broad clean streets of the great cities spoke of order and prosperity; the rhythm of the national pulse was strong and clear."

Such growth, such efficiency was unequalled in the world's history. But the people were unsatisfied. They hungered for more—a world-empire was their dream—if not in the West, why then in the East, where a much dreamed of railway from Berlin to Baghdad should carry their teeming millions to new lands beyond the frontier of the Rhine. A "place in the sun" was necessary to the rapidly increasing population.

They were ready to preserve peace on their own terms—holding that the German should be so strong by land and sea that he could "swagger down the High Street of the World, making his will prevail at every turn."

To this end the Kaiser had followed a consistent policy, which in the end led his country to the "slippery slope down which she glided into war."

9. PEACE OR WAR

"War is the national industry of Prussia."

—Mirabeau.

"The whole of Germany is charged with electricity," reported an American after a visit to Berlin in the summer of 1914. "It only needs a spark to let the whole thing off."

The spark was struck sooner than he imagined—struck in Bosnia, lately one of the Balkan States.

It was Sunday morning the 28th of June 1914, and the little town of Serajevo, the capital of Bosnia, which had but six years ago passed under the rule of Austria-Hungary, was early astir, for was not the Archduke Francis Ferdinand, nephew of the Emperor and heir to the throne, coming to inspect the troops in the capital?

Sad, lonely, unpopular, and profoundly distrusted at his uncle's court at Vienna, the Archduke and his wife were received by the Governor of Bosnia and his staff, and motors conveyed the royal party through the uneven streets of the strange little city.

It was crowded with people, of whom not a few were Serbians, and known to be full of conspirators, but no precautions were taken to safe-guard the Archduke. Progress was slow, and the motors made their way leisurely to the Town Hall. Suddenly a black parcel fell into the open hood of the Archduke's car. As he pushed it off it exploded, slightly wounding his aide-de-camp. The would-be assassin was arrested. The Archduke was very angry.

"I am here to pay you a visit," he expostulated to the Burgomaster, "and I am greeted with bombs. The fellow will get the Golden Cross of Merit for this," he added bitterly.

An address of welcome was then read as arranged, and the Archduke made his formal reply. He then proposed to drive to the hospital to visit his wounded aide-de-camp. They tried to dissuade him. The streets were narrow and no proper guard could be kept. There was danger in the air.

But the heir to Austria's throne was determined, and a motor containing the Governor, the Archduke, and his wife started forth. It was not yet eleven o'clock and the car was moving slowly along, when a young man pushed his way through the motley crowd and fired three pistol shots into the car.

The Archduke Francis Ferdinand, hit at close range, fell dead. His wife, a bullet in her side, died a few minutes later. The whole city was suddenly hushed and awed, and the Burgomaster, in an impassioned speech, laid the ghastly crime at Serbia's door. Europe was startled and horrified by the news, but no one dreamed that the dramatic events of that June morning were to rank among the most fateful moments of history.

Silence fell, the whole situation was full of mystery and misgiving. The Emperor Francis Joseph left Vienna, the Kaiser started on a yachting cruise, the French President left Paris to fulfil his engagement with Russia. But in the light of future events, the event was of world-wide importance.

It was 20th July 1914 when the historic meeting took place between Tsar Nicholas II. and the President of the French Republic. The great warship France brought the head of the French State to the little harbour of Peterhof, where the Tsar, on his favourite little yacht *Alexandra*, was awaiting him. To the mingled strains of the "Marseillaise" and the "Russian National Anthem," Monsieur

Poincare stepped on board the yacht to be received by the Tsar of all the Russias. For three days, banquets, receptions, reviews and other brilliant functions were the order of the day. At the end of the time, the news flashed through Europe that "the visit which the President of the French Republic has just paid to His Majesty the Emperor of Russia has given the two friendly and allied governments an opportunity of discovering, that they are in entire agreement in their views on the various problems which make for peace and the balance of power in Europe."

Monsieur Poincare had not reached France on his way home, when on 23rd July a thunderbolt fell.

Austria-Hungary had presented an ultimatum to Serbia!

A reply was demanded within forty-eight hours. According to the ultimatum, the matter under dispute was not given as the Archduke's murder—that crime only ranked as one of a long list of offences,—but Austria demanded no less than the submission of all Serbia to her Protectorate. As she had annexed Bosnia and Herzegovina six years before, so now she willed that Serbia should come under her sway. Her whole existence was at stake. The fact that Germany was behind Austria and had given her a free hand in this matter created a dangerous situation. The eyes of Europe were turned on Serbia. What would she reply? She accepted eight of the ten Austrian conditions, hard though they were, and her submission was almost complete.

But Austria was demanding unconditional surrender—she would be satisfied with nothing less, and Serbia could give no more.

It was Sunday, 26th July, when Austria began to move her troops toward the Serbian border, and Serbia began to mobilise. Two days later Austria declared war, and soon Serbia's capital, Belgrade, was occupied by Austrian troops.

It still seemed possible that the struggle should be localised and no other countries entangled in the dispute. But behind Serbia stood Russia—and Russia could hardly be expected to sit still and watch that independent little State become subject to Austria or perhaps to allow other Balkan States to be swallowed up without an effort to save them!

She began to mobilise on the Austrian frontier. Now indeed alarm broke forth in Europe. If Russia fought for Serbia and Germany for Austria, what would be the attitude of the other Powers? There was the Republic of France and the Commonwealth of Britain to be reckoned with yet. "As soon as there is a ten to one chance in favour of war, we must forestall our opponent and commence hostilities without more ado, and mercilessly crush all resistance." Such was the opinion of young Germans in 1913.

That Germany had been preparing for a European war for years past is certain. Secret preparation, the creation of giant guns, the arming of the German colonies, all pointed to war sooner or later, and, "While the world still slept and others were busy with securities for peace, the German General Staff had selected its maps for the coming battlefields." France, they realised, was "awake but unready; and the British people were neither ready nor awake," neither would they believe in the "creeping shadows "and "broken lights "of the European situation.

The Kaiser returned from his cruise to Berlin, shocked at Russia's war-like preparations. He at once telegraphed to the Tsar begging him to keep the peace.

The Tsar replied by begging the Kaiser to restrain Austria from her hasty action in avenging the murder of the Archduke. "In Russia," he added, "the indignation, which I share, is tremendous." A more serious communication between the two countries followed. Unless Russia would stop all military preparations, Germany would be forced to declare war on her in support of Austria. All hopes of peace gradually waned, and on 1st August 1914, Germany declared war on Russia.

Meanwhile Great Britain was working desperately to prevent the war spreading. The intervention of Russia on behalf of Serbia involved her new ally France. If only France and Great Britain could remain neutral, the conflict might yet be localised. But the skies were swiftly darkening, the war fever was spreading. On 3rd August Germany declared war on France.

What was the attitude of Great Britain? What of the Entente Cordiale? All hopes of peace now diminished with Germany's next move. The Kaiser suddenly announced his intention of marching through Belgium to France, and if Belgium opposed his advance, the army would "hack" its way through to Paris.

Now long ago in 1839 a treaty had been signed in London by which Austria, France, Great Britain, and Russia had promised to guarantee the independence of Belgium as a neutral State. Germany knew this treaty and only recently the German Minister of War had announced, "Germany will not lose sight of the fact that Belgium is guaranteed by international treaty."

Germany was about to disregard the treaty.

Albert, King of the Belgians, made a supreme appeal to England. Would she too disregard this treaty? England replied that she felt the treaty to be a sacred obligation, advised Belgium to resist by force any German invasion, and promised support.

> "So, when the challenge rang,
> 'The War-Lord comes; give room!'
> Fearless to arms you sprang
> Against the odds of doom.

> "So strong in faith you dared
> Defy the giant, scorn
> Ignobly to be spared,
> Though trampled, spoiled, and torn."

"We are in a state of necessity, and necessity knows no laws," replied the Germans to the expostulation of the Powers. "But the wrong that we are committing we will try to make good as soon as our military goal is reached," they added.

The hours passed heavily on. The Germans were already at the Belgian frontier, when the British ultimatum was presented requesting Germany to withdraw her troops at once.

It was late on 4th August. Germany had not expected this of England.

"Just for a scrap of paper Great Britain was going to make war on a kindred nation, who desired nothing better than to be friends with her."

If a solemn compact was to be treated as a scrap of paper, who could ever believe in the honour of England again?

Her honour was at stake.

The Germans refused to withdraw their troops. At midnight, 4th August 1914, Great Britain too had joined in the World War.

> "Come the three corners of the world in arms
> And we shall shock them. Nought shall make us rue
> If England to itself do rest but true."

10. THE WORLD AT WAR

"What of the faith and fire within us
Men who march away,
Ere the barn-cocks say
Night is growing grey,
To hazards whence no tears can win us,
What of the faith and fire within us
Men who march away!"

—T. HARDY (1914).

"We draw the sword with a clean conscience and clean hands," proclaimed the Kaiser on 4th August.

There was not a country involved in the War that did not feel precisely the same.

Ranged against one another now on that summer day were the Central Powers, Germany and Austria-Hungary on the one hand, Belgium, Russia, France, and Great Britain on the other.

The Germans had every reason to expect an easy and overwhelming victory over their opponents. They had the largest number of perfectly trained soldiers in the world, the best brains in Europe had worked at their military organisation, their war material was first-rate and inexhaustible. Their allies—at present their only allies—had an army organised on the German system of universal military service—now obedient to the German High Command.

Their opponent, Russia, had vast numbers of soldiers, but they were ill-equipped and only half-armed. What wonder their collapse came early in the war when the Russians had but one rifle among three soldiers to Germany's three rifles to every soldier! Nevertheless national enthusiasm ran strong, and all classes seemed to unite in a marvellous wave of patriotism despite internal troubles. The Grand Duke Nicholas, the Tsar's uncle, was made General of the Forces, with orders to "force his way to Berlin at the earliest possible moment and at any cost."

"Germany is the bitterest enemy of Russia," said the people. A great ceremonial took place at the Kremlin Palace at Moscow, and amid a dense throng of their subjects the Tsar and Tsarina, together with their four daughters and the little Tsarevitch (carried in the arms of a Cossack), made their State entry.

"From this place, the very heart of Russia, I send my soul's greeting to my valiant troops and my noble allies. God is with us."

The Tsar's words, spoken with great emotion, were answered by a great burst of cheering. It was one of the last times that the ill-fated Russian Imperial family were seen and cheered by their Russian subjects.

The story of Russia's part in the war will be told later.

Monsieur Poincaré did not reach Paris after his visit to Russia till 29th July. On the eve of possible war, France found herself ready for every effort and every sacrifice. M. Poincaré drove through Paris amid vast multitudes of people who had but one cry, "Vive la France."

The fighting machine which France set in motion on the outbreak of war ranked second among the world forces. In numbers she was inferior to Germany—her strength lay rather in the quality of her soldiers than in their equipment. Among officers and men was a spirit of comradeship which made for strength.

The strength of Great Britain lay more on the sea than on land.

> "The fleet of England is her all-in-all,
> And in her fleet her Fate."

Only on 18th July had King George reviewed his fleet off Portsmouth. It was the most powerful fleet ever assembled, numbering some 200 ships, drawn up in eight lines—no less than twenty-two miles of ships manned by 70,000 officers and men. For the first time the forces afloat were supplemented by seaplanes, aeroplanes, and airships. These would naturally have dispersed when the Review was over—but the war cloud was hanging over Europe, and the fleet was held together in case of emergency. As events rushed forward, and efforts for peace seemed growing fainter, the British Grand Fleet received orders to leave Portland, and in the evening of 29th July they put to sea.

"We may picture this great Fleet with its flotillas and cruisers, steaming slowly out of Portland Harbour, squadron by squadron, scores of gigantic castles of steel wending their way across the misty shining sea, like giants bowed in anxious thought. We may picture them again as darkness fell—eighteen miles of warships running at full speed and in absolute blackness through the narrow Straits into the broad waters of the North Sea."

Before war was actually declared, the First Fleet had vanished into the mists of the unknown. The efficiency of the Fleet alone made possible the transport of the British Expeditionary Force to France within a few days of the declaration of war.

"Come over and help us" was the cry of the French, for the Germans were already thundering at their gates.

On Sunday morning, 9th August, the first two transports landed the first British soldiers at Boulogne amid wild enthusiasm. At the time complete silence reigned, but we know now something of the 360 trains a day that carried our troops away to France—indeed no less than 1800 special trains ran in five days while embarkation was at its height, until by 25th August some 100,000 British stood on French soil.

"A finer fighting unit never entered the field."

Every kind of ship was used for crossing the Channel, from the ordinary cross-channel steamer carrying some 300 passengers to the giant Atlantic liner carrying thousands. From Southampton, Dover, Folkestone, Newhaven a constant stream of men, horses, food, and equipment passed ceaselessly for nearly a fortnight, while aeroplanes kept watch above and two little submarines crept into the Bight of Heligoland to ensure the safety of the soldiers. Not one accident occurred.

> "Not for passion or for power,
> Clean of hands and calm of soul,
> England, at this awful hour
> Bids her battle-thunders roll."

Had the Expeditionary Force together with the armies for Home Defence been all that Great Britain could offer as her contribution to the Great War, it would indeed have been disastrous. But during these opening days of the war, the whole British Empire rose to a loyalty and patriotism unsurpassed in the world's history.

"No man," it has well been said, "can read without emotion the tale of those early days in August, when from every quarter of the globe there poured in appeals for the right to share in our struggle."

If the Germans had thought of the British Commonwealth as a "weak alliance of independent nations," loosely knit together, so loosely that, at the first touch of serious danger from outside, it would fall to pieces and crumble away, if they considered that the Empire was getting heartily sick of the Imperial connection, they knew now that it consisted of a true union of hearts bound together in a common cause—a newly revealed Brotherhood.

They were—

> "Children of Britain's island breed
> To whom the mother in her need
> Perchance may one day call."

Canada flung her resources open in the cause of the Allies. Men of the western plains, the best shots and the hardest riders on earth, journeyed ' great distances to offer their services. Large sums of money were ungrudgingly given, and Canadian steamships were offered for transport. "Every public man in Canada played his part."

Australia and New Zealand with their system of national service were not behind Canada in loyalty. They gave freely of their sons, and nowhere on the battlefields of Europe could a finer set of fighting men be found.

British and Dutch in South Africa heard the war cry, old officers of the Boer commandos hurried to London to enlist with young men from Rhodesia, and amid immense enthusiasm General Botha placed himself at the head of South African troops for a campaign against German South-west Africa.

But perhaps the most wonderful sacrifice was that of India, which "took the world by surprise and thrilled every British heart."

"What orders has my King for me?" asked one Maharaja after giving his troops, his money, and his private, jewels.

When on 4th August news that England must fight reached

India, a resolution was instantly passed of "unswerving loyalty and enthusiastic devotion to the King-Emperor." Rulers and Princes gave unflinching support, and a number were selected for personal service in the field. The veteran Sir Pertab Singh would not be denied his right to serve the King-Emperor of India, and although seventy years of age he rode forth to the Great War, his nephew—the Maharaja of sixteen—accompanying him with other Rajputs and Chiefs. Never in India's history had such a muster been known.

But they hardly realised at this moment of enthusiasm what suffering their service would entail. For many of them the voyage was terrible; they had never seen the sea, and the great English ships filled them with alarm. They came to a country where climate, language, people, customs were all new. They had never been under heavy shell fire, they had no experience of high explosives, and the exposure to all the latest scientific developments in the art of destruction added indescribable suffering.

The Dalai Lama of far-off Tibet—the "Roof of the World"—offered a thousand Tibetan troops, with a message to the King that throughout the length and breadth of the land, Lamas were praying for the success of the British arms.

Well might King George exclaim, "Nothing has moved me more than the passionate devotion to my throne expressed by my Indian subjects, and their prodigal offers of their lives and resources of the Realm."

> "Never King of England
> Had nobles richer and more loyal subjects."

11. THROUGH BELGIUM TO FRANCE

*"When all was ready to their hand,
They loosed the hidden sword
And utterly laid waste a land
Their oath was pledged to guard."*

—R. KIPLING.

There had never been any suspicion of unfriendliness on the part of Germany towards Belgium. King Albert and the Queen Elizabeth had paid an official visit to Potsdam in 1910, which was returned soon after by the Kaiser and the Empress with their young daughter. Brussels had spared no efforts in her decorations for the royal guests, and the Kaiser, after looking down on the market-place from the balcony of the Town Hall, had exclaimed to the Empress: "We did not expect anything so beautiful."

Did Belgium, which had not been seen by William II. for thirty-two years, seem then a possible addition to the Great Empire ever hungering for expansion? The Belgian army had long been on a peace footing, but with war-clouds hanging over Europe, universal service had been introduced. Still the army was small and incapable of defending the little Belgian kingdom, through which her great neighbour now proposed to march. On the evening of 2nd August, in a highly confidential Note, came a request from Germany for leave for German troops to pass quietly through Belgium, using the citadels of Liege and Namur for operations against France. Belgium must desert her trust as a "neutral" to allow the troops to pass; her territory will be restored after the conclusion of peace, and indemnity for any damage that may be done. On the other hand, if Belgium uses armed resistance, she will be treated as an enemy. Twelve hours were given for the reply. It was enough. There was no hesitation. The answer went swiftly back. Belgium would defend her neutrality sword in hand. It was a brave decision, for with a small and ill-equipped army there could be little chance of success against the mightiest war machine in the world.

"I have faith in our destiny," said King Albert, who with the Queen and their three young children—Princes Leopold, Charles, and the little Princess Marie José—passed into the National Palace amid a scene of great enthusiasm.

"A country which defends itself merits the respect of all. That country will not perish. God be with us in this just cause. Vive la Bélgique indépendante."

And the King placed himself resolutely at the head of his little army as their Commander-in-Chief.

The later position was well illustrated in an English paper. The King stands in the midst of ruins, alone, uplifted, and the Kaiser stands near —triumphant and confident.

"So you see—you've lost everything," he is saying, to which the King of the Belgians, young and resolute, replies, "Not my soul."

But the foe was already across the frontier. On the night of 1st August, after their declaration of war with France, German motor-cars followed by trains had burst through the neutral Duchy of Luxemburg, and the following day loud explosions, caused by the destruction of bridges, told the Belgians that the Germans had crossed their frontier, and were making straight for the fortress of Liege, which barred their way to Paris. They did not rate Belgian valour high, and anticipated an easy task.

Speed and secrecy were of supreme importance before the English and French were ready. They were not prepared for the strong defence put up at Liege by the Belgians. The first German assault failed, and the enemy was driven back with heavy loss. The following day the southern forts were pierced, and on 7th August, the city fell; but the German army had been held up for two days, Belgians still commanded the railways, and the German troops could not proceed.

The Germans now revealed to the world one of the great surprises of the war. Quickly they brought up their huge cannon, moved about easily on broad wheels, to positions already prepared in secret. The forts commanding the railway were shattered to bits, but precious days had been lost by the foe. It was already 15th August when the great German army marched towards Namur—Namur held by the Belgians to be impregnable. But the great fortress fell in thirty-six hours, and the road into France was now open.

The collapse of Namur was the "first resounding success of the Germans in the war."

Across the French frontier now swept the vast host of German soldiers—over a million strong,—such an army as the world had never seen before. Perfect in every detail, the grey-clad soldiers pressed on in a never-ending stream, accompanied by their terrifying engines of destruction.

With pride and confidence in his own perfect war machine, it were small wonder if the Kaiser had really said the words ascribed to him, and ordered his troops to "annihilate the contemptible little English army."

Contemptible in size it may have been, but matchless in deeds of valour.

The situation in England was serious enough when Lord

Kitchener agreed to become Secretary of State for War in response to popular clamour.

"There is no army," he had asserted on his appointment. And indeed it was common knowledge that the first small Expeditionary Force under Sir John French—leader of cavalry—was wholly inadequate for the colossal task before them.

Lord Kitchener saw the truth at a glance, and it is to his undying fame that he created the wondrous new armies which were to fight and die in a cause in which all believed.

"YOUR KING AND COUNTRY NEED YOU.
A CALL TO ARMS.

So ran the posters throughout the land those hot August days in 1914. "An addition of 100,000 men to His Majesty's Regular Army is immediately necessary in the present grave National Emergency. Lord Kitchener is confident that his appeal will be at once responded to by all those who have the safety of our Empire at heart."

Four days after the declaration of war, a hundred thousand men joined the colours; within a fortnight they were in camp—the first of the new armies to be enrolled, housed, fed, clothed, trained, armed, and equipped with guns, rifles, and ammunition, henceforth to follow to France the Expeditionary Force now on its way. Every man of this first force knew his duty well. Each active service pay-book contained a reminder of what was expected of him.

"You are ordered abroad as a soldier of the King to help our French comrades against the invasion of a common enemy. You have to perform a task which will need your courage, your energy, your patience.

Through Belgium to France

"Remember that the honour of the British army depends on your individual conduct. It will be your duty, not only to set an example of discipline and perfect steadiness under fire, but also to maintain the most friendly relations with those whom you are helping in this struggle.

"Be invariably courteous, considerate, and kind. You are sure to meet with a welcome and to be trusted; your conduct must justify that welcome and that trust."

> "Do your duty bravely,
> Fear God,
> Honour the King."

Soon long lines of these khaki-clad men were moving slowly along the dusty white roads of France, enthusiastically welcomed by their French allies. In physique and equipment they were unrivalled. It is said they went as young happy boys going to the unknown war in a "sporting spirit as though it were a game."

What if their own marching song of "Tipperary" was to become later the death dirge of that gallant host!

> "Think that when to-morrow comes
> War shall claim command of all,
> Thou must hear the roll of drums,
> Thou must hear the trumpet's call.
> Now, before they silence ruth,
> Commune with the voice of truth.
> England! on thy knees to-night
> Pray that God defend the right."
>
> SIR H. NEWBOLT *(THE VIGIL).*

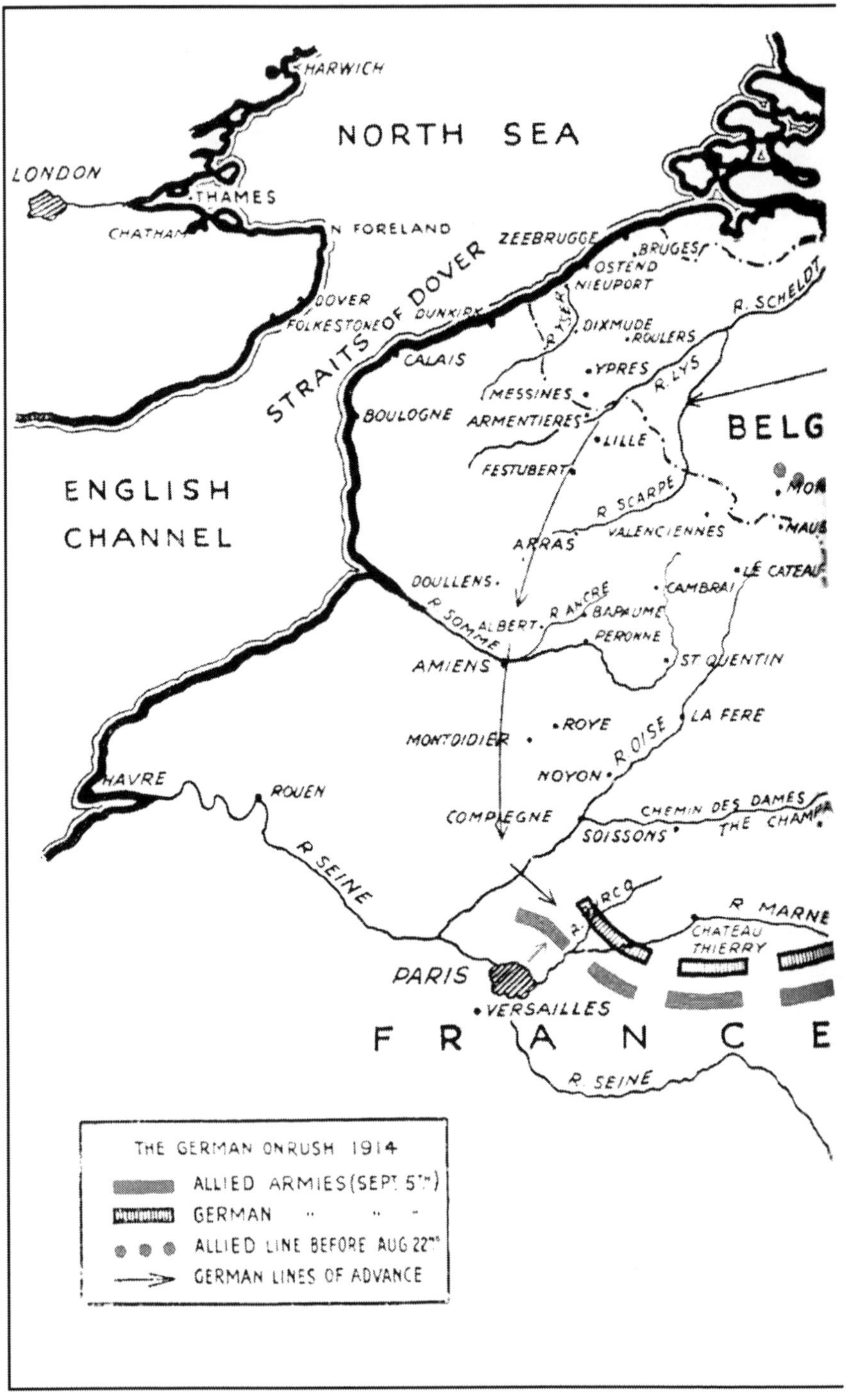
HARWICH
NORTH SEA
LONDON
THAMES
CHATHAM
N FORELAND
ZEEBRUGGE
BRUGES
OSTEND
NIEUPORT
STRAITS OF DOVER
DOVER
FOLKESTONE
DUNKIRK
R. YSER
DIXMUDE
ROULERS
R. SCHELDT
CALAIS
YPRES
R. LYS
MESSINES
BOULOGNE
ARMENTIERES
LILLE
BELG
ENGLISH CHANNEL
FESTUBERT
R. SCARPE
VALENCIENNES
ARRAS
LE CATEAU
DOULLENS
CAMBRAI
R. ANCRE
R. SOMME
ALBERT
BAPAUME
PERONNE
AMIENS
ST QUENTIN
LA FERE
ROYE
MONTDIDIER
R. OISE
NOYON
HAVRE
ROUEN
COMPIEGNE
CHEMIN DES DAMES
SOISSONS
R. SEINE
R. MARNE
CHATEAU THIERRY
PARIS
VERSAILLES
FRANCE
R. SEINE
THE GERMAN ONRUSH 1914
ALLIED ARMIES (SEPT. 5TH)
GERMAN " " "
ALLIED LINE BEFORE AUG 22ND
GERMAN LINES OF ADVANCE

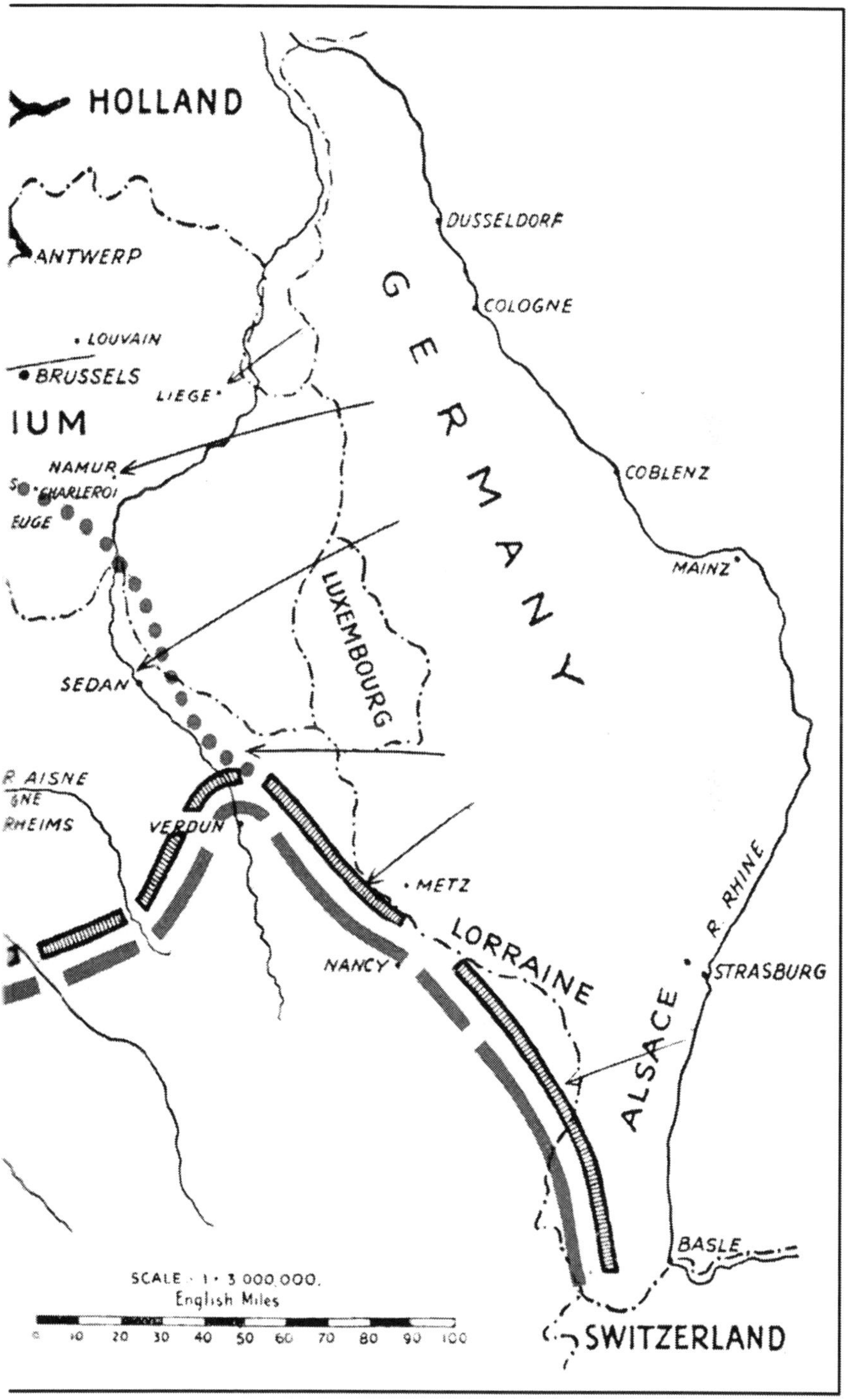
HOLLAND
ANTWERP
LOUVAIN
BRUSSELS
IUM
LIEGE
NAMUR
CHARLEROI
SEDAN
R. AISNE
RHEIMS
VERDUN
METZ
NANCY
LORRAINE
ALSACE
R. RHINE
STRASBURG
BASLE
SWITZERLAND
GERMANY
LUXEMBOURG
DUSSELDORF
COLOGNE
COBLENZ
MAINZ
SCALE · 1 · 3 000,000.
English Miles
0 10 20 30 40 50 60 70 80 90 100

12. TOWARDS PARIS

(Retreat from Mons and Battle of the Marne.)

"These in the hour when Heaven was falling,
The day when earth's foundations fled,
Followed their mercenary calling
And took their wages and are dead."

THE CONTEMPTIBLE ARMY, 1914.

A hundred and fifty miles in eleven days, along dusty roads under a fierce midsummer sun, was a creditable enough achievement for the young British troops. On 18th and 19th August they had reached the Belgian frontier, and a few days later found them in position at Mons. Their information was scanty and misleading. They did not know that Namur had fallen, that the remains of the Belgians had taken refuge in Antwerp, and that Brussels was in the hands of the Germans, who were rapidly descending on Northern France in a two-hundred-mile line. The French army under General Joffre—rushing also to the help of Belgium—met the great German army at Charleroi on the Meuse, where they were speedily defeated, and obliged to retreat.

They had indeed been in retreat for some twelve hours, when on Sunday, 23rd August, the British troops about Mons came into action, still in complete ignorance of the disaster at Charleroi, ignorant too of the strength of their foe. True, a British aeroplane had reported that roads to the north were "alive with advancing Germans," but all forecasts with regard to numbers proved wrong.

With the first streak of dawn came the first German shells,

and one by one the British guns "roared into action." Growing fiercer and yet more terrible, the battle lasted till late afternoon. The British position was grave, but not critical. Then at 5 o'clock came a telegram from General Joffre. It contained grave news to Sir John French. It told of the fall of Namur, of the French defeat at Charleroi, of the overwhelming forces against them of some 200,000 men, with another 40,000 working round. It was indeed a perilous position. The British troops were alone and isolated in the face of an enemy twice its strength.

"It seemed a force marked out for destruction."

Sir John French did not hesitate; only one course was possible, bitter as it was—immediate retreat. The order was given to fall back, and the now famous retreat from Mons began. For part of the army, it began at once; for many, not till 25th August, a day of glaring summer heat, changing to a downpour of rain at night, when the British army, disappointed and weary, faced southward for the long hard march back through France. Battle-worn and exhausted though they were, there could be no rest until they had extricated themselves from the immediate danger of being surrounded and cut off by the ever-pursuing Germans. On they marched, by different highways, ever toward Paris, now through drenching rain, now through intolerable dust and the glare of the mid-day sun, throwing away their packs, coats, rifles—all that impeded them. Added to this, part of the army had to turn and fight the oncoming foe at Le Cateau in a position from which escape seemed impossible. Here some eight thousand lost their lives. The remainder were ever hard-pressed, and with great empty gaps in their ranks—the places of those who had marched so hopefully with them but a short week ago—they pushed bravely onwards.

"Splendid you passed, the great surrender made,
Into the light that never more shall fade."

Day after day it was the same story, "March on," until at the last point of human endurance, the British soldiers staggered on, to the distant sound of German guns.

It was not until 2nd September that the whole army met again, at the crossing of the Marne, a tributary of the Seine. Their losses had been heavy; out of the 100,000 men who fought at Mons, some 15,000 never returned.

It has been said that "the old Regular Army, led by the best in the land, saved the national honour in the acutest crisis in history, and ceased to exist in the doing of it."

But if the retreat from Mons is a glorious page in the history of the British army, the advance after the retreat was no less remarkable, enabling the French to win the battle of the Marne, which saved Paris and changed the whole course of the first year's campaign.

The French army, too, had been hastily retreating toward Paris, after their disastrous defeat at Charleroi, before the advancing foe, for the German armies were even now rushing down upon the French capital.

"If the Generals would allow it, the men would run to Paris instead of walking there," remarked one of the German leaders of the great invading force.

As it was, indeed, their rate of progress was little less than thirty miles a day, for their leaders, Von Kluck and Von Billow, knew that a decisive victory over the Allies must be gained at all costs, and that soon.

Joffre and his armies, backed up by the British Allies, were ready for the Germans; the defence of Paris was already arranged, when on 5th September Joffre issued his famous order: "The hour has come to advance at all costs, and to die where you stand rather than give way."

It was the eve of the battle of the Marne, and the German army was likewise stimulated to great deeds: "The objects of our long and arduous marches have been achieved. The principal French troops have been forced to accept battle. For the honour of Germany, I expect every officer and man to do his duty unswervingly and to his last breath."

Von Kluck and his great army had crossed the River Marne and his patrols had reached the Seine. "It was a bright and solitary glimpse of the river on which stood the capital of France."

For, owing to the unexpected rally of the British troops after the retreat, owing to lost time in Belgium—a priceless asset to the Allies,—the French were able to place an undefeated French army across the German path, so that any siege or encirclement of Paris became impossible. So Von Kluck hurriedly changed his plans, and with that change of plan, Paris was saved. The French Government had already left the capital for Bordeaux when the first shots of the battle of the Marne were fired.

It was Sunday, 6th September. Soon the fighting became desperate, and for the next three days the battle was to "swing and sway" from side to side. The French—with everything at stake—were fighting for their lives and their land, but at times it seemed as though Von Kluck's desperate efforts would defeat the Allies once more. At one moment the French position was indeed desperate; unless reinforcements could be brought up, disaster seemed certain. It was a dramatic move when all the taxis in Paris were suddenly commandeered, filled with soldiers, and rushed forty miles to the fighting line. The tragic situation was saved. Saved, too, was Paris. For, suddenly and unexpectedly, aeroplanes reported that the Germans were retreating. They were moving by many roads to the north. The famous Prussian Guard, hitherto undefeated and held to be invincible, were falling back in haste.

Back across the Marne they scrambled, pursued by the Allies, hustled over some thirty miles of the same country across which they had so triumphantly marched but a short time since—till they reached the river Aisne—the first chill of disaster on them. The great German surprise, so long, so carefully planned, had failed; the blow had been turned aside. In a far-flung contest every man in the French and British armies had done his appointed task, and earned a share of the triumph.

But it was the unconquerable spirit of France that achieved the victory of the Marne—"the most decisive incident in the Great War."

13. A RACE TO THE SEA

"This England never did, nor never shall
Lie at the proud foot of a conqueror."
—SHAKESPEARE (*KING JOHN*).

The German bid for Paris had failed. For the first time since the days of Napoleon a Prussian army had been turned and forced to retreat. From river to river they had been pushed back across thirty miles of French land so lately conquered, till, crossing the river Aisne, they destroyed the bridges, and entrenched themselves on the sloping ground of the farther side.

Behind their lines lay the richest coal and iron-ore district in France, and the Germans were well aware that the supply of munitions to their Allies must henceforth be stopped.

It was a perfect position chosen by the Germans for their stand. They were up some two miles from the banks of the river Aisne on the crest of the high ground beyond, and, hidden in trenches, they commanded the river crossings for a distance of fifteen miles. The Allies, facing them on the opposite side of the Aisne, did not realise the immense strength of their position, neither at this time could they even dimly see that the Germans were about to dictate to them a new form of battle by compelling them to accept trench warfare.

On 12th September the two great armies stood face to face—the deep unfordable river Aisne, swollen with recent rain, rolling between them. The bridges were down, and on the heights facing the Allies, stood a formidable foe commanding every possible crossing.

And then, as if some miracle had happened, two days later most of the soldiers were across the river and established in positions from which the Germans were unable to drive them. It is impossible to over-rate the wonderful work of the engineers, who, under heavy fire and soaked by a cold driving rain, managed in that short time to build nine bridges and restore five already destroyed!

To gain the height and drive off the Germans was now the main object of the Allies. It was an almost hopeless task. Though equally matched in numbers, the German position was wellnigh impregnable, and a "deadly fire mowed down the ever-advancing troops in merciless masses. Now gaining, now losing, courageous beyond all belief, attack after attack proved unavailing." Day after day the armies fought desperately. The Allies could not take the heights, the Germans could not drive back the Allies. To make matters worse, a steady downpour of rain churned the ground into a deep chalky mud which filled the eyes, ears, throats of the soldiers, plastering their clothes and mixing with their food.

And still

> "The thundering line of battle stands,
> And in the air Death moans and sings."

During one short week no less than 2000 men were dead or dying daily, so endless was the supply of machine-guns, so terrible the deadly German shell fire.

Gradually the attacks died down, degenerating into sullen tench warfare, until early in October the losses on the Aisne had amounted to nearly 13,000 men.

A new development was now at hand. It was 3rd October,

and the deadlock on the Aisne still continued. But there was danger brewing in the North, and these men must be replaced by others. Very quietly one night, under cover of darkness, the British stole out of their trenches on the hill-side, crossed the Aisne once more, and made northwards before their departure and the arrival of others had been discovered. The retreat was masterly—a very "triumph of transport organisation."

A spell of beautiful autumn sunshine had followed the heavy September rains, and the sun shone out of a clear sky as the men marched or rode from the battlefields of the Aisne towards the French coast.

The object of this move was an attempt to join up the existing French line to the Belgian army, which was still holding out in Antwerp; and if this was successful, to push on and attack the German lines of communication which led back through Belgium into Germany. A whisper had grown to a rumour, and rumour to a certainty, that they were after the Channel ports.

After the occupation of Brussels, the King and his Government had retired inside Antwerp—held to be impregnable. Defences were strengthened, and here the last stand of the Belgians was to be made. Everything was at a standstill, docks and quays empty, the port deserted, the town isolated. News came of advancing Germans, of how Louvain—a peaceful city of students at the famous old University, one of the oldest and most illustrious centres of learning in Europe, with a famous library—had been captured. Then came the first Zeppelin raid, when for the first time in history a great civilised community was bombarded from the sky in the darkness of the night.

"Count Zeppelin," the Kaiser had said with triumph, "is the greatest genius of the century."

Meanwhile the great German siege guns were on their way to

Antwerp, and by 27th September a bombardment of the southern forts had begun. All day long the great guns pounded the forts, and there was no rest for the Belgian garrison within the city.

"When victory comes to our armies, what will remain of hapless Belgium?" said the poor King as the siege continued.

Still, amid the thunder of the guns, the citizens felt the forts were impregnable, and eagerly looked for British help.

Now acute anxiety was felt in England for the condition of Antwerp, and a British naval division had been despatched. But it was too late to save the city. On 7th October, the great guns had drawn nearer, and the citizens knew that Antwerp was doomed. Every possible means of exit was thronged by frantic and agonised crowds carrying away their household goods. They crowded into steam yachts and pleasure boats, fishing smacks, and even rafts, to reach the coast. They crossed the Scheldt by the bridge of boats and fled to Holland in an agony of suffering and fear, while the great guns roared on behind them and shells whistled overhead.

On 9th October all was over—the great bombardment ceased, and the Germans gaily entered in, only to find that one of the proudest cities of Europe lay empty and desolate.

England received hundreds and thousands of Belgian refugees. "Haggard, grey-faced people of all classes of society, in all forms of raiment," poured into Folkestone to be fed and cared for during these early months of war.

And the King? During the next four years, while the Germans were in possession of his country, he lived near Ostend.

"No monarch of the great ages more nobly fulfilled the ideal of Kingship. He raised Belgium to the position of a Great Power, if moral dignity has any meaning in the world."

"We owe everything to the King," said a desolate refugee who had lost everything. "He has made of our farmers and tradesmen a nation of heroes. When the war is over, he will rule over a broken land and a very poor people, but for all that he will be one of the greatest Kings in the world."

> "O tried and proved, whose record stands
> Lettered in blood too deep to fade,
> Take courage! here in our hands
> Shall the avenging sword be stayed
> Till you are healed of all your pain,
> And come with Honour to your own again."
>
> —OWEN SEAMAN (1915).

14. THE WESTERN FRONT—YPRES

"On the grim fields of Flanders, the old battle plain,
Their armies held the iron line round Ypres in the rain,
From Bixschoote to Baecelaere and down to the Lys river."
—Margaret Woods (The First Battle of Ypres).

When two armies meet each other face to face, and are in such positions that neither can dislodge the other, the commanders endeavour to strike a blow round one or other of the enemy's flanks. Such was the position in France at the end of September 1914. The Germans, forced back, as we have seen, at the height of their first victorious rush, were now firmly established on a line stretching along the Chemin des Dames above the Aisne, north of Rheims, Verdun, and Nancy, to the mountains of Switzerland. The Belgian army was still at this time holding out in Antwerp.

General Joffre, the French Commander-in-Chief, began by sending troops north of the Oise against St. Quentin. The Germans sent troops to meet them, and so move and counter-move followed each other until the line of stalemate was extended as far north as Lille.

In all these moves, and in all future movements on the Western Front, it must be remembered that the Germans held the great advantage of being on the inside of a circle, whilst the Allies were on the outer edge. Therefore any move between two points on the line was shorter for the Germans, and whichever side made the move first, the Germans always had a slight advantage in the all-important matter of time.

Whilst the French were extending their line to the north,

the British Expeditionary Force, successfully withdrawn from their positions on the Aisne, were hurrying round behind them, with the object of filling the gap between them and the Belgians in Antwerp, and of attacking the German lines of communication, which led back into their own country through Belgium. A British naval division had also been sent hurriedly to Antwerp, and the 7th Division was working its way to the same place through Flanders.

Up to this time the Germans had been too busy with the battles of the Marne and the Aisne to take any measures against the fortress of Antwerp; but now, threatened by the advance of the British and French towards the Scheldt, they decided to capture this place.

As had happened at Liege and Namur, the fortifications of Antwerp proved no match against the gigantic new guns with which Germany had surprised the world, and on 8th October the Belgian army left the city, and the Germans took possession next day, as has already been described.

The gallant little Belgian army, led by King Albert himself, having stood up so bravely against the first onslaught, was now driven from its last stronghold. Some of them, together with a part of the British Naval division, were forced into Holland, while the remainder, hard-pressed and outnumbered, retreated down the Belgian coast, past Ostend, until they reached the River Yser. The line of this river had to be held at all costs, or Dunkirk and Calais would be threatened, the last thin strip of Belgian soil lost, and the armies at Ypres surrounded. On 10th October British ships, carrying powerful long-range guns, came rushing across the North Sea to Nieuport, and soon across the dreary, rain-sodden sand-dunes heavy fire descended on the Germans. Day after day the Belgians held on, but on 2nd

THE BATTLE LINE
AT END OF 1914.

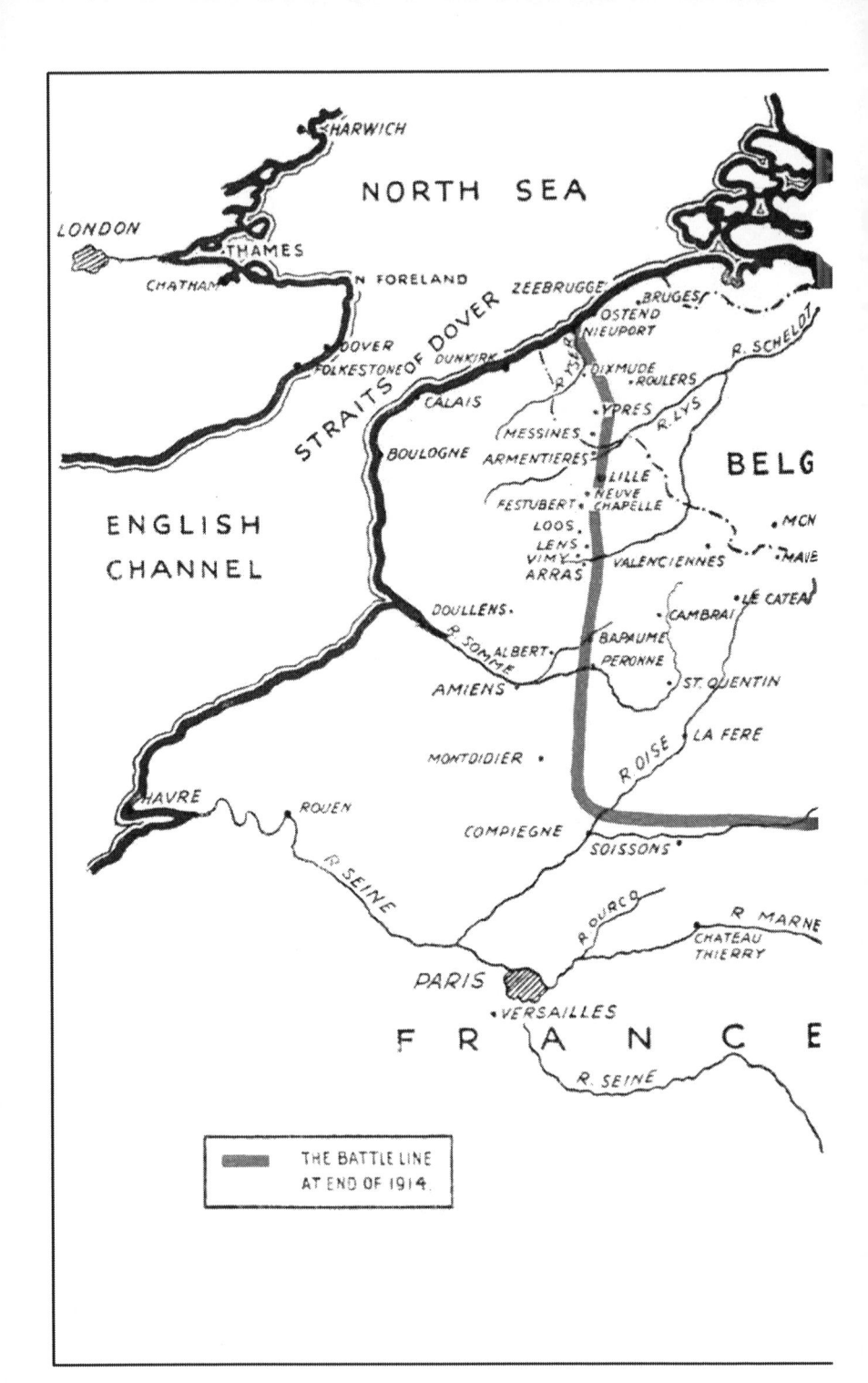

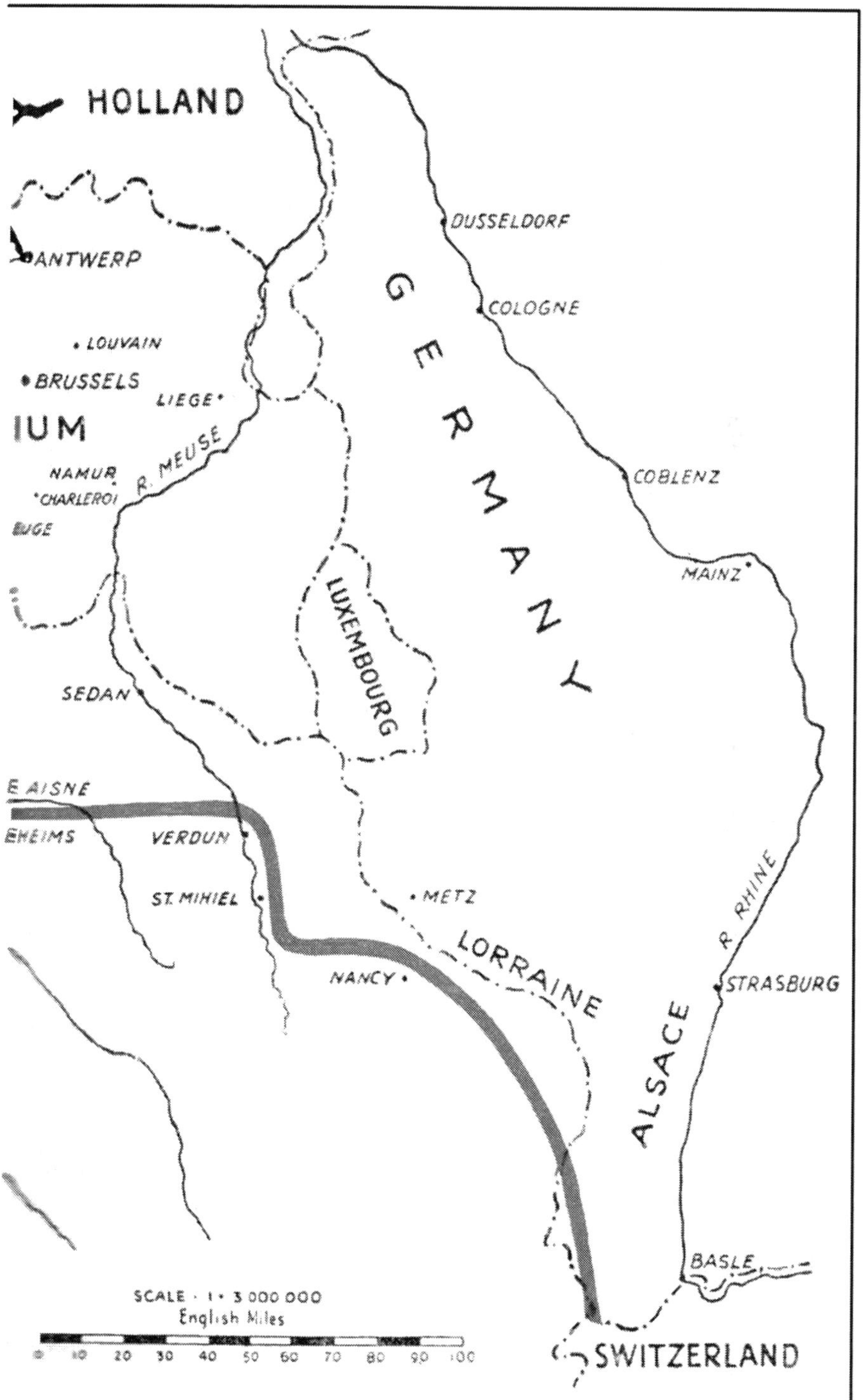

HOLLAND
ANTWERP
LOUVAIN
BRUSSELS
IUM
LIEGE
NAMUR
CHARLEROI
R. MEUSE
SEDAN
E AISNE
RHEIMS
VERDUN
ST. MIHIEL
NANCY
METZ
LORRAINE
LUXEMBOURG
GERMANY
DUSSELDORF
COLOGNE
COBLENZ
MAINZ
R. RHINE
STRASBURG
ALSACE
BASLE
SWITZERLAND
SCALE · 1 : 3 000 000
English Miles
0 10 20 30 40 50 60 70 80 90 100

October the Germans succeeded in crossing the river between Dixmude and Nieuport: then they played their last card, they opened the lock-gates and flooded the country. The Germans, caught in the rising tide, were drowned; some escaped, many were made prisoners. The attack had failed. The Kaiser, who had been watching the coast operations, shut up his glasses and turned away.

Meanwhile the British were still advancing in Flanders, but this advance was met by the unexpectedly strong attacks of the German armies released by the fall of Antwerp. Once again outnumbered, and in a hazardous situation, the British began to be forced back.

It was only now, their dreams of reaching Paris shattered on the Marne, and their eyes opened by their successes in the north, that the Germans began to consider seriously the capture of the Channel ports—Calais, Dunkirk, and Boulogne. They realised the tremendous value of this stretch of coast-line; how by commanding the Straits of Dover, they would cut off the English Channel from the North Sea, and at the same time sever the link by which the British Army was maintained in France. The Channel ports, the gateway to England, would be a richer prize than Paris, and the winning of them became, for the time being, the aim and object of the German Higher Command. The Kaiser appeared himself to conduct operations.

Deadlock had now been reached along the whole front from Switzerland to the vicinity of Neuve Chapelle, and the door had been locked to the advancing Germans from Dixmude to the sea by the inundations on the Yser. There remained only the gap, in the centre of which lay Ypres. Ypres, the old capital of Western Flanders, with its famous Cloth Hall, was a landmark amidst the flat lands of Flanders, and was destined to become the centre of the greatest clash of arms the world had ever seen.

Behind the gap lay Calais, and in the gap stood all that remained of the British Expeditionary Force. They had enjoyed no rest since 23rd August, had lost many of their best officers and men, and knew that the armies, preparing in England, were not yet ready to take the field.; and that, if they gave way now, those armies might never have the opportunity of doing so. The Germans, feeling the approach of winter, and not having yet won any material success in the West, collected all their available troops and flung them against this thinly held line. Their progress at first was slow, for the British fell back stubbornly, fighting every inch of the ground, but on 31st October they reached a line just east of Ypres, from which they could not in safety retire another yard, and the order went forth, "Hold on at all costs!"

The situation was critical in the extreme: the line was so thinly manned that it might well be broken at any point at any moment, and there were no reserves behind with which to mend the breach. But the line held, and on 1st November some relief was afforded by the arrival of French troops.

The rain came, and the whole countryside became a quagmire of mud: movement became almost impossible, and the men in the trenches fought under the most terrible conditions. Reduced to a minimum in numbers there was no possibility of any system of relief, but wet through, worn out, and often without food, the men held out against the almost continuous attacks of the enemy.

On 11th November these attacks culminated in the onslaught of the Prussian Guard, when the flower of the German army, under the eyes of their Emperor, flung themselves against the

British Line. With magnificent dash and amazing valour, they poured over the British positions, only to be mown down in thousands by rifle and machine-gun fire. Again and again they advanced, and again and again they recoiled.

"So all day long the noise of battle roll'd."

But the line held!

After the failure of this grand attack, the German efforts grew weaker, until about 17th November the first battle of Ypres may be said to have finished, and the fighting waned away in utter exhaustion. The casualties in human life during the six weeks were little short of 300,000 men, including both sides. Nearly 10,000 fell on 11th November alone.

The positions were now consolidated on both sides, and the deadlock was complete from Switzerland to the North Sea.

Such is the story of the formation of the Western Front, brought about partly by the enormous number of men employed, and partly by the undreamed-of power of modern weapons. The old methods of war were gone, although the principles remained unchanged, and both sides spent the winter in devising new methods with which to overcome the novel situation. For it was realised then, and never lost sight of by the men who knew, that ultimate victory must be sought on the Western Front.

15. THE RUSSIAN ALLIES

"Once to every man and nation comes the moment to decide,
In the strife of Truth with Falsehood, for the good or evil side."
—LOWELL (THE PRESENT CRISIS).

So far, only the fighting between France, Great Britain, and Belgium against Germany and Austria-Hungary has been mentioned.

But Russia was one of the Allies also ranged against the "Central Powers," and until the great tragedy occurred that broke up her immense Empire, she played her part in the world war.

Her reasons for declaring war have already been told. The war was popular. Up to this time the great country had been divided; it was hopelessly divided again later on; there was the Russia of the Tsar and Government and the Russia of the people.

With the bursting of the war-cloud, Russia was united, and her enthusiasm uplifted the land with an almost religious fervour. Great enthusiasm greeted the appointment of the Grand Duke Nicholas as Commander-in-Chief of the Russian army. He was the Tsar's uncle, a man of iron will, standing 6 feet 3 inches in height. His orders were to "force his way to Berlin at the earliest possible moment and at any cost."

By the third week in August 1914, some two million Russian soldiers were under arms, and as the gigantic battles in Northern France developed, the Allies looked to Russia to invade Germany, and compel her to turn her attention to the East instead of the Western Front.

There was an idea that the great Russian army —the "Russian steam-roller," as it was called—would sweep like some tidal wave toward Berlin, and so relieve the very critical situation.

Now, to invade Germany, two tasks lay before the Grand Duke Nicholas. He must drive the Germans out of East Prussia on the north and the Austrians from Galicia on the south, for in between lay Poland, and Poland at this time was every man's land.

Part of her was Russian, part German, part Austrian. And one of the most tragic features of the whole tragic struggle was that Poland—once a first-class European Power—was now divided against herself. True, soon after the outbreak of war, Russia made a bid for Poland.

"Poles," ran her famous declaration, "the time has come when the dream of your fathers and forefathers will at length be realised. The time has come for the resurrection of the Polish nation and its fraternal union with Russia. May the frontiers which have divided the Polish people be broken down. May it once more be united under the sceptre of the Russian Emperor. With open heart, with hand fraternally outstretched, great Russia comes to you. The morning star of a new life is rising for Poland."

But this ambition was never realised, for just a year later, the Germans marched into Poland's capital, Warsaw, and there was no more any talk of a Russian Poland.

The route planned by the Grand Duke Nicholas was the northern one by East Prussia. For the first ten days or so, the Russian army marched on towards Berlin with entire success, driving back the Prussian inhabitants of the country.

With the news brought back by fugitives that East Prussia was in the grip of the Russian foe, the Germans became alarmed. Was not East Prussia the seat of the old Prussian kings, and Konigsberg the capital, in the far-away days when Berlin was but a fishing village? Hastily the Kaiser appointed General von Hindenburg, an old soldier sixty-seven years of age, now living in retirement, to command this region. He knew this part of the country well, and might be trusted to baffle the Russians in a land unknown to them. There was no time to be lost. The situation was critical. Skillfully the old General laid his plans. While one Russian division was marching due east toward Berlin, another was marching in a northerly direction to meet it. Hindenburg now planned to prevent a meeting.

At the right moment, when the Russians were marching carelessly forward confident of success, Hindenburg turned them and drove them back into the woods of Tannenberg, back into unknown country full of swamps and lakes and marshes of black mud. There was no way of escape in that trackless land, and soon regiment after regiment became engulfed in treacherous swamps. Men, horses, guns were sucked down into the abyss. For days the agony continued, till on 26th August some 90,000 prisoners fell into the hands of the Germans, with guns, horses, ammunition, and all that had escaped from the waters of the lakes about Tannenberg.

The German victory was complete. Hindenburg was the hero of the hour, and Berlin was wild with joy. The Kaiser raised him to the rank of Field-Marshal, a stepping-stone to the near future, when he should become Commander-in-Chief of the whole German army in the East.

But though disaster had ended the Russian advance to Berlin, and the £20,000 raised in Russia for the first soldier to enter Berlin was never won, yet there still remained other openings for a Russian advance.

The invasion of Austria proved an easier task, for the Russian troops were now advancing across the frontier into Galicia—a vast plain stretching to the Carpathians, with its two great fortresses of Przemysl and Lemberg—both vital to the defenders of Austria. It was at Lemberg on 1st September, while yet Berlin was rejoicing and Russia mourning over the battle of Tannenberg, that Austrians and Russians met, and the critical battle of Lemberg was fought and won by the Russian troops, who captured great quantities of stores and a large number of Austrian prisoners, and entered the city in triumph.

The Grand Duke Nicholas telegraphed the good news to the Tsar, and all over Russia solemn thanksgiving services took place. People spoke of their "invincible Russian armies," and expected daily to hear that the Russians were in possession of Vienna!

As September advanced, the Russians invested the great fortress of Przemysl, and Russian armies were threatening Cracow—the capital of Galicia. The Kaiser again became seriously alarmed, for was not Cracow the very gateway to Vienna and Berlin?

Hindenburg was again to the fore. The situation demanded a master mind, for the Austrians in Galicia were hard hit. He decided on a counter-stroke. Warsaw should be attacked to save Cracow. Now Warsaw, the capital of the Russian province of Poland, lay on the banks of the river Vistula. All through the shortening days of October desperate fighting took place. Driven back once, the Germans again advanced with redoubled vigour. Hindenburg wanted the Polish city as a Christmas present for his Kaiser, but the Russian defence was too strong for him. Christmas found Russians and Austrians entrenched in untakable trenches much as Germans and French had met in a deadlock on the Western Front.

"The winter stalemate, long delayed in the East, had at last arrived."

16. ON THE HIGH SEAS

"Grey wakes the daybreak, the shivering sails are set
To misty deeps,
The Channel sweeps—
O Mother, think on us who think on thee,
Earth—home, birth-home, with love remember yet
Thy sons in exile on the eternal sea."

—SIR H. NEWBOLT (OUTWARD BOUND).

But before that first war-Christmas dawned, what had been happening to the Grand Fleet which had put to sea with the first whispers of the war? And what of the German navy that had been so feverishly building these last fifteen years or more?

In command of the British Grand Fleet was Sir John Jellicoe, a brilliant seaman of vast experience, who, on his flagship the Iron Duke, the largest Dreadnought afloat, had a task before him of colossal magnitude. Of Sir David Beatty, who had just received knighthood from the King on board the Royal yacht after the Review of the Fleet on 20th July, as Vice-Admiral, the public knew but little as yet. Commanding the German Fleet was Admiral von Tirpitz—a man whose energy and will-power had made the navy what it was—the second in the world. But it was untried as yet. And to keep this German battle squadron lying idle at its moorings behind Heligoland round about the mouth of the Kiel Canal was the task of the British at this point of the war.

"The Admiral of the Kiel Canal," as von Tirpitz was lightly named by his foes, was passively awaiting developments at this

FINLAND
L. LADOGA
(CHRISTIANIA)
(OSLO)
NORWAY
SWEDEN
STOCKHOLM
GULF OF FINLAND
(ST PETERSBURG)
(PETROGRAD)
SCALE 1:10,000,000.
English Miles
0
50
100
200
300
NORTH SEA
JUTLAND BANK
DENMARK
COPENHAGEN
BALTIC SEA
GULF OF RIGA
RIGA
HELIGOLAND
KIEL CANAL
KIEL
HAMBURG
STETTIN
DANZIG
KÖNIGSBURG
KOVNO
EAST PRUSSIA
RUSSIA
TANNENBERG
HOLLAND
BERLIN
GERMANY
WARSAW
PINSK
BREST-LITOVSK
LODZ
BELGUIM
COLOGNE
DRESDEN
BRESLAU

PRAGUE
CRACOW
LEMBERG
PRZEMYSL
CARPATHIAN MOUNTAINS
GALICIA
FRANCE
R. RHINE
L. CONSTANCE
R. DANUBE
VIENNA
BERNE
SWITZERLAND
BUDA-PEST
AUSTRIA
HUNGARY
ODESSA
RUMANIA
TRENTINO
CAPORETTO
GORIZIA
R. PIAVE
TRIESTE
VENICE
FIUME
BOSNIA
BELGRADE
BUCHAREST
R. DANUBE
ITALY
ADRIATIC SEA
HERZEGOVINA
SERAJEVO
SERBIA
NISH
BULGARIA
BLACK SEA
CORSICA
MONTE-NEGRO
SCUTARI
SOFIA
ROME
DURAZZO
ALBANIA
TURKEY
CONSTANTINOPLE
SARDINIA
SALONIKA
AEGEAN SEA
ASIA MINOR

juncture. "If the German ships do not come out, they will be dug out like rats in a hole," said the British sailors.

It was near the end of August. The Expeditionary Force were in full retreat from Mons, and bad news of the German advance clouded the country, when Sir David Beatty led his ships into the Bight of Heligoland and took the enemy by surprise.

At midnight on 26th August, a small party of submarines under Commodore Roger Keyes crossed from Harwich for the Bight of Heligoland, the plan being to tempt out enemy ships to where British battleships awaited them. Though the morning was calm and still, and the rock of Heligoland rose out of a morning mist, the submarines succeeded in luring out some German destroyers and cruisers, while the British cut them off from their base. Before 8 o'clock in the morning a battle began, and during the long August day, when the early morning mist had given way before the hot summer sun, the battle continued. By 12 o'clock Sir David Beatty had sent some battle cruisers at full speed through a "mine-strewn and submarine-haunted sea." Their timely arrival decided the battle. In the early afternoon victory lay with the British, whose losses were slight. The Germans had lost three ships and a destroyer, while seven hundred of her sailors perished. Admiral von Tirpitz's son was saved from drowning, and made prisoner.

> "As rose the misty sun
> Our men the North Sea scanned,
> And each rejoicing gun
> Welcomed a foe at hand,
> And thundering its delight,
> Opened its mouth outright,
> And bit them in the Bight,
> The Bight of Heligoland."

On the High Seas

Although the British had not fought since Trafalgar, the great spirit of the navy had never shone more brightly, and officers and men stood on their ships till they sank. And while it is true that most of the naval events of the war cluster round the waters of the North Sea, in addition to the Grand Fleet were other ships keeping guard in other waters throughout the world.

Especially dangerous were the ships of a German battle squadron in far Eastern waters under Admiral von Spee, a bold commander, an efficient seaman, a chivalrous foe. Until it was hunted down and put out of action, the Australian and New Zealand troops could not be transported with safety to the fighting fronts, where they were badly needed. It was the first duty of the British navy to free the seas of this danger and to keep open the trade routes.

In command of the North American station was Admiral Cradock with a small squadron, which included two old battleships—long obsolete—and some slow cruisers with guns of an old-fashioned pattern. With such equipment he took up the chase of von Spee with his four ships, all with powerful guns and fast of speed.

Off the South American coast of Chile, Cradock fell on his German foe. He knew but too well that the odds were against him, and that speed and equipment were bound to tell. But in a "spirit of devotion to a desperate duty," he set out to engage some of the best ships in the German fleet.

It was 1st November, late afternoon, a day of bright sunshine, but a high wind and a rough sea made all ships roll heavily.

"To the east was the land, with the snowy heights of the Andes fired by the evening glow. To the west burned one of those flaming sunsets which the Pacific knows, and silhouetted against its crimson and orange, were the British ships."

Cradock from the south, just round Cape Horn, and von Spee from the north moved towards one another, till by seven in the evening the ships were separated only by seven miles of foaming sea. The sun had gone down when firing began, and shell after shell hit the old battleship Good Hope, on which stood Admiral Cradock with his 1650 officers and men. Presently an explosion shook the ship, white flames "mingled with the stars" and leapt high into the air. The doomed vessel with its heroic Commander and entire crew went down. Not one was saved. Other ships came into action, but the victory was with von Spee. It has been said such a defeat was without parallel in British naval history. Cradock's instructions were confused. At the last he might have made his escape, but he was not that man, and perhaps the words chosen for his monument in York Minster furnish an explanation—

> "God forbid that I should do this thing,
> To flee away from them;
> If our time be come, let us die manfully for our brethren,
> And let us not stain our honour."

There was only one course of action open to the British—to retrieve the disaster of Coronel as soon as possible.

A new Commander was found in Admiral Sturdee. With two battleships taken from Admiral Jellicoe's Grand Fleet and other fast cruisers, Admiral Sturdee sailed, arriving at the Falkland Islands on 7th December. He decided to coal there and then go round Cape Horn in search of von Spee.

Early on the morning of the 8th, von Spee suddenly appeared from the direction of Cape Horn, quite unconscious of the nearness of the foe. By eight o'clock in the morning the Admiral had heard the news, orders were given to get up steam with all haste, and soon the British ships were pursuing the Germans with their vastly superior force. By mid-day the British ships were gaining, further flight was impossible, and von Spee made ready for battle—a battle the result of which was but too certain. "Ever since Coronel he had had a sense of impending doom, and had known that the time left to him was short."

By mid-day British guns were pounding the German flagship, which sank later in the afternoon, carrying down von Spee and his two sons. The bright morning had turned to a wet afternoon, and as the wet night closed in, the battle died away.

"The defeat of Cradock in the murky sunset off Coronel had been amply avenged "by the death of von Spee in the ice-cold waters off the Falkland Islands.

Both Admirals—English and German—had fought well. They had died as sailors die, without a thought of surrender. But naval success does not lie entirely with courage or even good seamanship. It lies, as the sea battles of Coronel and Falkland Islands show, with those "who think ahead in terms of mechanical force."

> "So long as the sea-wind blows unbound,
> And the sea-wave breaks in spray,
> For the Island's sons the world still runs,
> "The King and the King's Highway!'"
>
> —SIR H. NEWBOLT.

17. GALLIPOLI

"Through the Narrows of the Dardanelles and
across the ridge of the Gallipoli Peninsula lie some
of the shortest paths to a triumphant peace."

—WINSTON CHURCHILL (5TH JUNE 1915).

It was but three days before the battle of Coronel, while yet the fierce struggle for Ypres was nearing its crisis, and Russian victories were encouraging the English and French Allies, that news rang across Europe that Turkey had entered the War on the side of Germany.

The news was not unexpected. For many years past Germany had befriended the Turks; the Kaiser had visited the Sultan more than once in full state, and German officers had modeled the Turkish army on their own efficient lines.

For was not Constantinople her capital—at once the great military prize for which both Russia and Germany yearned? This entry of Turkey into the War convinced the British War Council that a blow must be struck somewhere in the Far East. The New Year 1915 dawned, and Winston Churchill, First Lord of the Admiralty, dreamed his dream of forcing the narrow Channel of the Dardanelles with British battle-ships, conquering the little Peninsula of Gallipoli, that "tongue of hilly land" some fifty-three miles long that lay over against the coast of Asia Minor. Then what could stay the ships from entering the Black Sea and realising his vision—"the downfall of a hostile empire, the destruction of an enemy fleet and army, and the fall of a world-famous capital."

"The struggle will be heavy," prophesied the dreamer, "the risks numerous, the losses cruel; but victory, when it comes, will make amends for all."

Victory never came in this sense. But the Dardanelles campaign will ever stand, "not as a tragedy nor as a mistake, but as a great human effort, which came, more than once, very near to triumph, achieved the impossible many times, and failed in the end as many great deeds of arms have failed." "This failure," adds an historian of the Gallipoli campaign, "is the second grand event of the war; the first was Belgium's answer to the German ultimatum."

Early in the New Year, British and French battleships were hurried to the great harbour of Mudros, in the island of Lemnos, some sixty miles from the Gallipoli Peninsula. By the middle of February quite a large fleet had been collected in this safe anchorage, and early one February morning eight ships opened fire on the forts at Cape Hellas, the nearest point of the Peninsular, while airships hovered overhead to report results. A few days later, led by the great new super-Dreadnought, the Queen Elizabeth, the bombardment was resumed. A terrific fire was poured on to the forts, but they were strongly defended by the Turks under German instruction, and the big naval guns could not silence them. Meanwhile the narrow channel between the land of Asia and the Peninsular had been mined by the enemy. On 18th March, the Allied ships made a fierce and determined attack on the shore defences. Right through the day the great guns boomed over land and sea from the Queen Elizabeth, the Lord Nelson and Agamemnon, the Inflexible, Prince George, and the Triumph, while four French battleships engaged the forts at close range, followed by more British warships. But suddenly, hidden by a cloud of smoke, one of the French ships struck a mine, and sank in three minutes with nearly all her crew. Soon after, two of the British battleships went down, and other ships were damaged. At twilight the great fleet steamed slowly out of the straits, followed by parting shots from the forts they had striven to destroy. Three first-class battleships and over 2000 men had been sacrificed in vain, and the hardest part of their task had not begun. There was consternation when the news reached England. It was then decided to send a land army to co-operate with the Fleet.

"But remember," said Lord Kitchener—"remember, once you set foot on the Gallipoli Peninsula, you must fight the thing through to a finish." It was five weeks before the troops arrived, by which time the Turks had constructed new defences with the help of German engineers, had concealed their heavy guns, put wire entanglement across miles of country, and converted the Achi Baba heights into an impregnable fortress commanding the land around. "Constantinople you may take, but Achi Baba—never," boasted the Turks with truth.

By the end of April, a strange medley of ships—from the obsolete battleship to the newest submarine—had collected in the harbour of Mudros, and the great black transports were beginning to move slowly out towards the Peninsula amid tumultuous cheering bearing their "freight of human courage." For the men knew what awaited them. They had to fight on a waterless land, 500 miles from a store; they had to take with them everything—guns, food, clothing, water, horses, and hospitals.

"No army in history has made a more heroic attack; no army in history has been set such a task; no other body of men in any modern war has been called upon to land over mined and wired waters under the cross-fire of machine-guns!"

Ship after ship crammed with soldiers moved slowly out

of the harbour, and felt again the heave of the sea. No such gathering of fine ships has ever been seen upon this earth. As they drew near the battleships, the men swung their caps, and cheered and cheered again, till the harbour rang with cheers. "It broke the hearts of all there, with pity and pride; it went beyond the guard of the English heart."

Dawn was early on Sunday morning, 25th April, as slowly and quietly in a calm sea the boats crept toward the land, and the men scrambled ashore.

The Battle of the Beaches almost defies description. On several beaches around Cape Hellas, notably V, W, and Y beaches, landings had been planned, but before the British landed, a, murderous fire blazed forth from hidden Turks on shore. Greeted by ten thousand shots a minute, men were shot dead before they set foot on land, many jumped overboard and swam ashore, others were swept away by the fierce current.

And right through that still spring day the great guns boomed from forts on land and battle-ships on sea.

The Australian and New Zealand Army Corps—Anzac will ever be their immortal name—landed farther to the north. In the darkness of the early morning they missed the appointed spot, and desperate was the fighting over rough ground and steep scrub-covered cliffs—men fell into unsuspected gulleys, but ever they pressed on under terrific fire over the broken hills. "Australia will be there," they shouted. Then "they dropped and fired and died," as company followed company to almost certain death.

By Tuesday, the 27th, the "impossible had happened." A footing had been gained at practically every landing; but nothing more, and the losses had been colossal.

Awful days and nights followed, but amid the unceasing

crash of artillery and the scream of many shells, followed by death-dealing explosions, little progress was made.

The great guns of Achi Baba dominated both land and sea. At the end of five weeks' fighting, more men had been lost than in the whole South African War.

Spring passed into summer, and the situation did not improve. The Turk was no mean foe. He was holding the gate of his capital Constantinople, and he had every advantage in men, arms, and position.

For the British the advance of summer brought increased discomfort. There was no shade; the sun beat pitilessly down on rock and scrub. The scarcity of water, a plague of flies and outbreaks of fever, sorely tried the troops as they sat in their stifling trenches day after day and week after week. "Never had our troops shown a more dauntless courage, a more complete devotion, or more stubborn resolution." Even their enemies were full of admiration. "These British are the finest fighters in the world," said the Turks; we have chosen the wrong friends."

The army was in great peril, difficult to reinforce, difficult to withdraw. The fleet was passive, and German submarines were beginning to attack the many ships supporting the Dardanelles operations.

Early in August, fresh troops arrived, and a great new surprise landing was made at Suvla Bay to the north of Anzac on the shores of the Aegean Sea. The day chosen for a great combined attack on the Peninsula, 6th August, was one of "airless and pitiless heat." To divert the enemy from the main attack on the Anafarfa hills, the Australians were to storm the Turkish fort on Lone Pine which commanded the main enemy water supply. Before that summer night fell, by sheer heroism, the position was won, and out of nine V.C.'s awarded for the

August battles in Gallipoli seven went to the conquerors and holders of Lone Pine.

For four days and nights isolated battles raged over the southern part of the Peninsula, battles fought in a blazing sun, with no rest, with little food and less water, and at the weary end but little had been gained. The sacrifice had been very great. No less than 30,000 casualties were reported, a quarter of the whole army—a loss even greater than at the first and second battles of Ypres.

The great battle of the campaign was over, and, despite incredible courage, it had failed, failed tragically, hopelessly. Sir Ian Hamilton was recalled, and the idea of withdrawing the troops was urged. Summer gave place to autumn, and Lord Kitchener himself visited the Peninsula and decided on evacuation. But the sufferings of the troops were not yet ended.

Towards the end of November, a blizzard of rain and sleet and wind rising to a gale swept over sea and land. With a bitter north wind and thunder, came rain more violent than any soldier on the Peninsula had ever seen. In a few minutes "every gully was a raging torrent and every trench a river." Bitter frost followed. Sentries were frozen dead at their posts, and the suffering of the troops reached the limits of human endurance. At Suvla alone there were 200 deaths from exposure, and no less than 10,000 sick had to be removed as a result of these few terrible days.

The evacuation was now hurried on during the spell of warmer weather that followed. It was a triumph of co-operation between army and fleet—an achievement "without parallel in military or naval history."

To remove large numbers of men, guns, and animals from positions commanded by the enemy was no light task. Night after night, showing no lights, the black transports crept in and out of Suvla Bay and Anzac Cove. There were 20,000 Turks on the battle front, but the warships kept up their usual bombardment, and the troops quietly embarked in perfect order.

Christmas still found British troops around Cape Hellas, but the New Year of 1916 found the same skilled withdrawal under cover of the night, until the whole Peninsula of Gallipoli was in the hands of the Turks with only our 50,000 dead left behind.

> "Great hearts are glad when it is time to give;
> Life is no life to him that dares not die,
> And death no death to him that dares to live."
> —SIR H. NEWBOLT (SACRAMENTUM SUPREMUM).

18. THE WESTERN FRONT— NEUVE CHAPELLE, LOOS

"They went with songs to the battle; they were young,
Straight of limb, true of eye, steady and aglow;
They were staunch to the end against odds uncounted;
They fell with their faces to the foe."

—LAURENCE BINYON.

To go back to the beginning of the year 1915, the situation on the Western Front was unaltered, but events which had been taking place elsewhere had a bearing on the programmes of the two sides. The entry of Turkey into the War on the side of Germany was, at the moment, affecting Russia more than any of the other Allies. Hindenburg, owing to his victories in East Prussia, had become the idol of the German people, and a power in the nation. Partly owing to his advice, and partly to a request for help from Austria, it was decided that the German plan of campaign for 1915 should be to hold the positions in the West, and to conduct a great offensive against the Russians in the East. The Germans accordingly strengthened their positions on the Western Front, and awaited with confidence any action which the Allies might take. That their confidence was not misplaced the story will show.

The battle line in France and Flanders from Switzerland to the North Sea was now 500 miles long, and of this great length the French held all except about fifty miles, but from this time onwards the British front was gradually increased. The original British Expeditionary Force had practically disappeared, but around its skeleton was being built up a new army from the ranks of the Territorials: Indian troops had already taken their place in the firing line, and suffered there untold miseries in weather such as they had never experienced before, and for which they were totally unsuited: the Dominions were sending the advance parties of those armies which they raised for the defence of the Mother Country and the Empire, while in England the vast citizen army, called for by Lord Kitchener, was being equipped and was training with an unparalleled keenness and intensity, in order to take its place in the far-flung battle line.

With all these preparations in progress, the Allies were full of hopes at the beginning of the year, and felt that they would be able to make such attacks as the Germans would be unable to withstand.

British plans were guided by the desire to control the Channel ports at all costs, and in order to make them more secure, Sir John French wished to make an attack northwards along the Flanders coast. General Joffre, however, was confident that he could break through the German line by making two attacks at the same time—one from Arras and one from Rheims. These two attacks were to work towards each other, and so cut off the German armies standing in the bulge between these points.

General Joffre's plan prevailed.

The first real test of the Allies' strength was the British attack at Neuve Chapelle. This gallant attack was launched on 10th March, and, under cover of what was then considered an intense bombardment, made some progress. But the strength of the German positions had been underestimated, and by 15th March the battle was over, without any gain having been attained which made up for the loss of life and material. The battle of Neuve Chapelle was described as being bigger than Waterloo, and yet in comparison with battles which were to come it was almost insignificant.

The next action was the second battle of Ypres. It began by a British attack on Hill 60. This was not a very big hill, but in that flat country it was high enough to be a view-point of great importance. The side which was in possession of any ground sufficiently high to give a view, was in a position to make things very uncomfortable for the others, because they were able to harass the movements of people well behind the lines, as well as those in the front-line trenches. Both sides were anxious to do away with this vantage-point, and they began burrowing into the hillside. The British won the race—though their miners could actually hear the German miners working above them—when on Saturday, 17th April, they exploded their mines, and literally blew the defending garrison off the hill. The Germans made many determined efforts to re-capture it, but the British held on with great tenacity against superior numbers, and under an intense bombardment.

Infuriated by the loss of this important point, and encouraged by their success in stopping the attack at Neuve Chapelle, the German Higher Command now decided to make another attack on Ypres and the road to the Channel ports.

For this purpose another scrap of paper was torn up—the Convention signed at the Hague on 29th July 1899; and at about 5 o'clock on Thursday afternoon, 22nd April, the poisonous gas cylinders were opened. The gas spurted out, and formed a greenish-yellow cloud, which drifted slowly before the wind towards the Allied trenches. Owing to its weight it remained thick on the ground, and there was no escape. There was no defence against the gas, and thousands of brave men endured the tortures of lingering, burning, suffocating death.

The Canadians, newly arrived and raw troops, found themselves at this critical point in the line, outnumbered by six to one, and faced by an unforeseen horror, which surpassed all the known horrors of war.

> "These were the men out there that night
> When Hell loomed close ahead,
> Who saw that pitiful hideous rout,
> And breathed those gases dread,
> While some went under and some went mad,
> But never a man there fled."

To the eternal honour of Canada they rose to the occasion, and saved the Imperial Army from a terrible disaster. At first alone, and then aided by British Territorial regiments, they held on against vastly greater numbers, poisonous gas, and an artillery fire of extraordinary violence, for nearly three weeks, when the German onslaught died down, and Ypres, the gateway to the Channel, was saved once more. Probably nothing in the war brings out more fully the words of Froissart, written in the days of Edward III.: "The Englishman suffers very patiently for a very long time. But in the end he pays back terribly!"

In May the British attacked at Festubert, and the French near Lens, but once again, after a successful beginning, progress was stopped to a great extent because of the lack of artillery ammunition. The British army was hopelessly handicapped in 1914, and for the first half of 1915, by lack of shells, a sure proof that Great Britain was not prepared for a war of aggression. During the summer months the industries of Great Britain and France were reorganised, and by September the supply of ammunition of all sorts had been greatly increased.

On 23rd September began the bombardment of the fronts

on which the British and French were going to attack—the former at Loos, and the latter in the Champagne country. This bombardment, the most intense yet seen in the war, was continued without a pause for from fifty to seventy hours, and it was confidently expected that, at the end of this time, a clear path would be revealed through the German defences. The Germans, however, had not been wasting their time: they had built up a series of positions one behind the other, which contained wonderfully constructed underground shelters, into which they retired during the bombardment. When this ceased and the Allies attacked, they were content to give up their forward positions, and appearing from their shell-proof dug-outs they met any further advance with a hailstorm of machine-gun and rifle fire, while their artillery brought down a terrific curtain of fire on to the positions which had been given up, and in which the attackers were struggling. Further progress was impossible, and in spite of the most heroic efforts on the parts of the Guards and the Territorials, all idea of a decisive result was abandoned by the end of the month.

Sir Douglas Haig now took over the command of the British Forces in France, a position which he held without a break until the Armistice. Sir John French came home to command the forces in Great Britain. He had shouldered the most tremendous responsibilities for over a year, and conducted two operations—the great retreat from Mons and the first battle of Ypres, which will always maintain a high place amongst the glorious exploits of the British Army.

One lesson from the fighting up to date was the unbelievable powers of endurance of man in a mechanical inferno. Many sound judges had considered that the human mind and frame would never be able to endure such a strain for more than a few months, and had based their calculations as to how long the war would last on this assumption. They were proved wrong.

The surprise of 1915 was the extraordinary strength of the German defensive system. It was realised that some new method of attack would have to be devised if the Western Front was to be broken in 1916, and the road to Berlin opened up.

19. THE TRAGEDY OF SERBIA

*"They paid the price to reach their goal
Across a world in flame."*

—R. KIPLING.

It was hardly likely that the restless Balkan States should remain neutral throughout the war. From the very beginning, constant and attractive offers for their sympathy and active help had been made by the Central Powers on the one side and by the Allies on the other. The first year of the war passed, and none of the Balkan States had as yet intervened.

True, Serbia had been fighting against Austria-Hungary since that day in 1914 when war was declared, and the old King Peter with his two young sons rode forth to do battle. It was known that Rumania, with her English Queen Marie, sympathised with the Allies, It was also a fact that Greece, with her German Queen Sophie, the Kaiser's own sister, was torn between the fighting factions. But with regard to Bulgaria—the Emperor Ferdinand had been a dark horse. Both sides claimed his attention; both thought they had gained it.

"Let us see how the struggle develops, and which side offers the highest price for our support." Such was the royal attitude.

The collapse of Russia and the failure of the Allies at Gallipoli confirmed Bulgaria in the view that the Germans would be victorious, and that it would be well to come in on the side of the victors. The country was divided. "War will lead to fresh disasters: it will not only ruin our country but your dynasty, and may cost you your head."

The royal reply was ignoble. "Neutrality," said the King, "has enabled us to bring the military preparedness of our army to such a pitch as has never before been reached." Serbia was an "eternal enemy," and "Russia's darling." Bulgaria began to mobilise, at the same time assuring the Allies of her "armed neutrality" as a measure of safety, although the capital Sofia was known to be full of German officers.

"The Bulgarian Government has taken up a position of armed neutrality," declared England, "to defend her rights and independence. Not only is there no hostility in this country to Bulgaria, but there is traditionally a warm feeling of sympathy for the Bulgarian people. If, however, the Bulgarian mobilisation were to result in Bulgaria taking the side of our enemies, we are prepared to give our friends in the Balkans all the support in our power without reserve and without qualification."

Suddenly the news rang through Europe that Bulgaria had thrown in her lot with Germany, and had decided on an invasion of Serbia in union with the Central Powers.

Early in October, General Mackensen had hurried south from Galicia to lead the Austrian forces against Serbia. It was not the first time since the outbreak of the war that Austria had invaded Serbia, bent on her annihilation. But their attempts to cross the Danube had been repulsed, and they had been hurled back across the frontier in confusion. Unfortunately this had exhausted the stock of Serbian munitions, and, hearing this, the Austrians had surged back, forcing the Serbians to evacuate their capital, Belgrade. This time it seemed as if the Austrians must succeed. To her fifty shells, the Serbians had but one. Everything depended on a grim stand till the promised munitions arrived.

"Heroes!" cried King Peter to his peasant soldiers in the trenches, fighting with their last remnants of ammunition, "you have taken two oaths: one to me, your King, and one to your country. From the first I release you; from the second, no man can release you. But if you decide to return to your houses, and if we should be victorious, you shall not suffer. As for me and my sons, we will remain here."

Not a man left his post. Ammunition arrived in time from the Allies, and the King entered Belgrade once more at the head of his heroic army. This defeat of the Austrian army by the Serbians appeared to the rest of Europe almost an impossible feat of arms. Enormous numbers of prisoners, guns, and war material fell into their hands.

But their trials were not yet ended. Their endurance was to be tested yet more highly. An epidemic of typhus now began to spread over the country. The Serbian soldiers, exhausted by their hard fighting, fell victims to it by the thousand. Hundreds fell and died by the roadside, and none could cope with the outbreak. Then the Serbians appealed to the Allies, who instantly responded to their call. France, Britain, and Russia sent out doctors and nurses, who worked day and night among the stricken people. Gradually science and heroism prevailed, but not till some 70,000 Serbians had succumbed to the terrible scourge.

Now, not one enemy alone, but four—Germany, Austria, Bulgaria, and Turkey— were invading their little land from various points. Again, in their distress, they turned to the Allies, who were even now hurrying to Salonika from Gallipoli ready for action. But one of Bulgaria's first efforts had been to cut off communication, and prevent any help reaching the Serbians from that quarter. Ignorant of this, the Serbians were buoying themselves up with hopes that British and French help would arrive in time to save them. Nish was decorated with bunting, and children stood with flowers to greet their friends. But they listened in vain for the guns that never came. They were alone, for Greece had failed them too. Greece, in honour bound to help Serbia in need, had repudiated the Treaty, and broken up for ever the Balkan League. The tragic drama of Serbia was beginning.

On 5th October the crash came with the bombardment of Belgrade by the Germans—one of the fiercest in the whole war. The capital was only defended by a small body of troops. Shells were bursting and German aeroplanes were dropping bombs on the defenceless people in the town. Overwhelmed by numbers, the Serbians fought desperately with the courage of despair, and when they at last evacuated the city, the German flag waved over a desolate scene of ruined homes. The Bulgarian army came into action on 11th October. It was 100,000 men stronger than the entire Serbian army, which had to face in addition 300,000 Germans and Austrians armed to the teeth. The position was desperate. As town after town fell into the hands of the enemy, the Serbians were pushed back and back westwards toward the great frontier mountains of Albania.

On 24th October, Uskub fell; on 5th November the Bulgarians took Nish; and with the union of the German army, the way to Constantinople was open. Masses of fugitives, to the distant sounds of the enemy's guns, fled from town and country by the only routes that were available. By the middle of November, winter had set in, and the great Albanian mountains and passes were deep in snow. The Serbians had lost heavily in men and guns, and only some 150,000 weary warriors were left out of her once heroic force. On the Albanian frontier, the last resolution was taken in the hour of storm and stress.

It must be unconditional surrender or further flight over the desolate snow-bound heights to the Adriatic coast.

On 24th November the decision was made. The King, the army, and Government refused to treat with the enemy—rather would they attempt the Albanian mountains.

The great Serbian retreat one of the great tragedies of the war—now began. It was "the exodus of a nation rather than the retreat of an army." There were two routes open—one through Montenegro to Scutari, and one through Albania to Durazzo. The roads were mere sheep tracks over the mountains. Waggons and horses had to be abandoned, food had to be carried, and the journey made on foot was across the endless ranges of snow-capped mountains—their peaks towering into cloud.

The old King, rheumatic and nearly blind, with the Royal Household and the Royal Guard, started himself on foot through the snow for the 120 miles to Scutari. Along every mountain track streamed long black lines of refugees—women and children, doctors and nurses, ministers, secretaries, consuls—the country's uprooted and exiled population. Snow fell as they tramped, and camp fires lit up the hillsides where the night was spent. Now they had to wade through streams of ice-cold water, now to creep along the edge of a precipice, where far below could be heard a rushing mountain torrent, now in blinding snow-storms, always with insufficient food and aching feet. The retreat is a confused story of cold and hunger and of heroic endurance—men dying by the wayside, others stumbling on silent with grief and misery. It is said a quarter of a million civilians and half the Serbian army perished on the retreat. But the long journey was over at last, and the remnants of what was once the Serbian nation were given headquarters at Corfu till the day of deliverance arrived.

"My soldiers," cried King Peter, "I yet believe in the liberty of Serbia. The dream of my youth, for which I fought throughout manhood, has become my faith in the twilight of my life. I am tired and bruised and broken from my struggle in life, but I must live to see Serbia free, and to see the victory of my country."

20. THE FALL OF KUT

"'O Captains unforgot,' they cried,
Come you again or come no more,
Across the world you keep the pride,
Across the world we mark the score."

—SIR H. NEWBOLT.

About the same time as the close of the tragedy of Gallipoli, another British expedition was ending in disaster. Again the expedition was directed against the Turks. Before even the bombardment of the Dardanelles had begun, German agents were busy around the Persian Gulf, which for long had been one of Britain's happy hunting grounds. And on the barren shores of the Gulf, across the waters from Bombay, British warships had ridden at anchor bringing to the Persians peace for many a long year past. Now India herself seemed threatened by Turkey, and a small British force was dispatched from India to the Turkish Headquarters at Basra—the old seaport of Mesopotamia at the head of the Gulf, the ancient home of Sinbad the Sailor.

Basra was successfully taken, and the British flag flew from the German Consulate there. But the Turks were still in force to the north, and it was decided to advance to Kurna, some 50 miles from Basra—the junction of the old Euphrates and Tigris—on to Amara, another 90 miles, and possibly to Kut, yet 150 miles upriver from Amara.

General Townshend was in India when he was given command of the expedition. Arriving at Basra toward the end of April 1915, he hurried up the Tigris for his first sight of Kurna. As far as the eye could see, the country was under flood, from which the Turkish positions stood up almost unapproachable. Townshend had a number of barges prepared and the troops were embarked. Then he manoeuvred his queer flotilla around the astonished Turks, and on 3rd June he was in Amara with much booty and many prisoners, while the Turks were in full retreat up the river. Kut lay beyond, and beyond Kut lay Bagdad—the prize of all this theatre of war. Townshend decided to push on to Kut, 150 miles up the river. Risks grew greater as the base was left farther and farther behind, and the lines of communication grew longer and longer. Transport was difficult; the floods had left large swamps; the sun shone pitilessly down, a blinding glare over the desert lands and across the blue waters. There was no shade to relieve the soldiers. But, in spite of fearful discomforts, the expedition moved on, now wading through water, now re-embarking in their shallow boats, through creeks and swamps and thick date groves under the cloudless sky, and ever tormented by swarms of flies.

On 26th September, Kut was attacked, and after a long and hard-fought battle, the Turks again retreated, leaving Townshend and his now somewhat reduced division in possession.

It were well had the expedition stopped there. But the thought of Bagdad lured them on—Bagdad, terminus of the highway from Germany and Constantinople, the great religious and trade centre of those parts. Townshend was now 300 miles from his base. His troops had suffered badly, and were weary with ten months' incessant fighting. That they should advance in this condition to the conquest of a mighty province of a still powerful empire might well seem a rash enterprise; besides which, the Turks were flushed with victory at Gallipoli, and by their side stood their German taskmasters to keep them to their work.

The Fall of Kut

"We have great need of a striking success in the East," ran a message from England. And General Townshend, mindful of his record of unbroken success, albeit with battle-worn and weary troops, moved onwards toward Bagdad.

The troops had to make the journey of 100 miles by land, but the autumn days were bright and clear, and the season well fitted for an advance. For some distance they marched without opposition, but when they were within some 30 miles of Bagdad, the unwelcome news came that 13,000 Turks had prepared a position at a place called Ctesiphon, which had been strongly fortified under German supervision.

Bravely enough the little Anglo-Indian force beat itself against the enemy's fortifications, until three days had been spent in battle, and aeroplanes reported that more and more reinforcements were reaching the Turks, who were losing heavily. Townshend had lost one-third of his men, and there was nothing for it but to retreat. With considerable skill he extricated his force, and fell back to Kut. On 2nd December, "the solitary minaret of Kut in the desert sky-line" appeared, and soon the remains of the little force, that but a month before had set out with high hopes, staggered back into the little town. "Never have I seen anything like the exhaustion of the troops after we reached Kut," wrote Townshend. "Eight hundred sick and wounded go down to-day. I am making Kut into as strong an entrenched camp as possible in the given time."

The time was indeed short, for a famous German General was in command of the Turkish army at Bagdad.

"I intend to defend Kut, and not retire any farther," said Townshend to his troops. "Our numbers are too few to put the enemy to rout. We have had 4000 men killed and wounded. You have added another page to the glorious battle roll of the army in India, and you will be proud to tell them at home that you fought at the battle of Ctesiphon."

So some 10,000 men, with provisions for two months, entrenched themselves at Kut, while the enemy placed their guns all round, and soon began a terrific bombardment. By 5th December, Townshend and his force were completely besieged, and the Turks barred the road to any relief force that might try to come. Attempts at relief there were, and on a large scale, but all, including that of Generals Aylmer and Gorringe during the months of January and March 1916, failed with grave losses.

While efforts at relief were causing thousands of casualties, the brave defenders within Kut were dying daily from actual starvation. Horse-meat was their main food, with a small amount of barley bread. Rice and sugar had come to an end in February, and milk had run out. Christmas Day was ushered in with a renewed assault, and 315 men were killed and wounded.

On 10th April, Townshend again addressed the troops: "The Relief Force has not yet won its way through. I must reduce our rations to 5 ounces of meal for all ranks—British and Indian. In this way we can hold out till 21st April. The whole British Empire is ringing with our defence of Kut."

At last the end came. It was 29th April, when a wireless message rang through the world: "Have hoisted the white flag over Kut." There was nothing left, but to surrender. It was a weary and broken force that now laid down their arms after holding out for 147 days. Kut had been held to the utmost limit of human endurance. Even the enemy realised this, and when General Townshend offered the Turks his sword in surrender, it was refused. He passed, as a prisoner of war, to Constantinople, where he remained till October 1918. But the rank and file were condemned to "unparalleled sufferings and barbarities" till half of them had perished.

The fall of Kut was but an incident in the great world struggle, but its tragedy lay in the unsurpassed heroism and endurance of the troops, and the disappearance of the whole valiant army into captivity.

RUSSIA
BLACK SEA
CONSTANTINOPLE
CAUCASUS MTS.
GEORGIA
TIFLIS
CASPIA
ARMENIA
AZERBAIJAN REP.
BAKU
TURKEY
KURDISTAN
R. TIGRIS
ALEPPO
MEDITERRANEAN SEA
SYRIA
MESOPOTAMIA
DAMASCUS
BAGDAD
CTESIPHON
PE
PORT SAID
JERUSALEM
GAZA
DEAD SEA
R. EUPHRATES
CAIRO
SUEZ
SINAI
AKABA
BASRA
ARABIA
PERSIAN
EGYPT
EL HEJAZ
R. NILE
RED SEA
MEDINA
JIDDAH
MECCA
SUDAN
KHARTUM
ERITREA
WHITE NILE
BLUE NILE
ABYSSINIA
ADEN

TURKESTAN
N SEA
TEHERAN
KABUL
AFGHANISTAN
RSIA
KANDAHAR
INDIA
GULF
GULF
OF OMAN
BOMBAY
ARABIAN
SEA
SCALE 1 : 20 000 000
English Miles
0 100 200 300 400 500

21. THE CAPTURE OF BAGDAD

> "No easy hope or lies
> Shall bring us to our goal,
> But iron sacrifice
> Of body, will, and soul."
>
> —R. KIPLING (FOR ALL WE HAVE AND ARE).

Kut fell at the end of April 1916. Its surrender had taught the military authorities, that long and careful preparation would be needed if Bagdad —the Turkish Headquarters—was to be captured. The man now chosen to carry out the work was Sir Stanley Maude. He had already fought on the Western Front, he had distinguished himself in the ill-fated expedition to the Dardanelles, and he had accompanied one of the hopeless expeditions to the relief of Kut. In August 1916 he arrived at Basra as the new Army Commander of the Anglo-Indian forces in Mesopotamia.

"It is a great responsibility," he wrote. "There are peculiar difficulties in connection with this campaign: there is the long line of communications, the shortage of river transport, the absence of roads and railways, the intense heat, floods, and difficulty of supplies." To get at the work, heart and soul, to overcome all obstacles, was Maude's great self-appointed task. He soon made his vigorous personality felt among the troops—despondent over the recent failure, weak and ill with the intense heat, tormented with flies and other discomforts.

For three and a half months he worked at lines of communication, the organisation of hospitals and ambulance, the

The Capture of Bagdad

production of wholesome food for the troops. Guns, ammunition, clothing, all had his attention. A light railway was laid, and little more than seven months after the fall of Kut, over 1000 steamships of sorts were plying up and down the Tigris. This river fleet was made up of boats from India, from the Nile, from Africa, and, among others, the Thames Penny Steamers were doing their bit too. It was not till December that the long period of preparation was over, and the time for action drew near. A steady stream of reinforcements had been moving up the Tigris for weeks past. Now the genius and foresight of the new commander were to be put to the test. Truly great events were at hand, though to the outside world it might seem that the situation on the banks of the Tigris and Euphrates called for no special attention.

The troops were in good health, partly owing to the cooler weather, and in good spirits. Aeroplanes reported the position of the Turks to be strongly entrenched round about Kut. No light task lay before Maude and his troops.

On 13th December the great offensive began. Fighting was long and strenuous, and heavy rains, causing a sudden rise in the Tigris with considerable floods, caused some delay. Early in the new year, further attack was possible. For ten days the Turks' resistance was stubborn, but steadily, foot by foot, they were pushed across the river Tigris. It was no time to pause. Day after day fighting went on, with terrible casualties on both sides. After two months of severe fighting, the army commander thanked the troops: "To all ranks of the fighting troops, my warmest thanks for their splendid work, and my congratulations on their brilliant success. The end is not yet, but with such co-operation and vigour animating all, our success is assured."

This was on 15th February. The most brilliant event in the

whole campaign was now to take place before the final recovery of Kut. The river Tigris had to be crossed—crossed at its highest in face of an enemy with a formidable array of guns and in strongly defended positions on the very scene of the siege of Kut. The enemy thought the crossing of the river wholly impossible—a feat that only madmen would attempt.

Just before daybreak on 23rd February, a detachment of English and Gurkhas ferried across the flooded river under machine-gun fire, which swept the shallow boats and inflicted heavy losses on the British.

"With unconquerable valour and determination" they worked on, till by afternoon the amazing bridge was ready for traffic. Soldiers poured across, and the Turkish army was in full retreat toward Bagdad, but fighting every foot of the way. It was a crossing to rank with the passage of the Aisne—the swollen Tigris being even a greater difficulty than the sluggish French stream. "Nothing could have been finer. It will take a very high place in the records of the British Army." Soon aeroplanes reported that every road was thronged with retreating Turkish troops. Kut was entered without opposition on 25th February. The disaster of ten months before was wiped out. With the crossing of the Tigris the whole situation was changed. The recovery of Kut, though of no importance in itself, appealed to people all over the world, and all eyes were turned to the next stage in the war.

The next fortnight was to settle the question of Bagdad. Although the Turkish army was in full retreat, they disputed every foot of the way with stubborn resistance, and the advance from Kut to Bagdad was a matter of unending hand-to-hand fighting amid a network of defences. By land and water the pursuing force pressed forward, "pushing on merrily," as their leader called it. Shortage of supplies demanded a momentary

The Capture of Bagdad

pause in the pursuit, but 5th March found the fleet and mounted troops pushing on, the army commander himself steaming up-river in a big paddle-wheel boat. On the 9th they were within seven miles of the city, and a blinding dust-storm made some delay. But two days later the defeated Turks, realising the game was up, deserted Bagdad absolutely demoralised.

The great day had come, and on 11th March, Sir Stanley Maude, the conqueror of Bagdad, stepped quietly ashore with his staff close to the British Residency to take possession. "The banks were lined on both sides with crowds of inhabitants, who applauded loudly, and seemed delighted that we had arrived," remarked Maude, the army commander. Soon, through the old North Gate, marched the victorious troops as they took possession of the famous old city of the Kaliphs. Tidings of the capture of Bagdad aroused enthusiasm throughout the Allied countries. It was the first great triumph since the battle of the Marne, and it had a far-reaching effect on the East. Congratulations from the King, from the Viceroy of India, from Grand Duke Nicholas of Russia, from Admiral Beatty, now in charge of the British Fleet, and others poured in to the army commander, to whose triumphant organisation the victory was due. Truly it was said of him that "each difficulty encountered served but to steel the determination to overcome it."

It was not till the surrounding country had been conquered and the Turks finally beaten at Mosul, that General Maude could settle down to consolidate his work. Specially did he attend to the medical service and hospitals. As the summer passed, the heat was intense, cholera broke out in Arab quarters, and the army commander insisted on the troops being inoculated. All that was possible was done for their comfort and well-being. But their chief worked hard, taking no thought for himself. The summer passed, and November came. Suddenly one evening toward the middle of the month the conqueror of Bagdad was stricken with cholera, of which in a few days he died. Simply he had lived and simply died. But never was grief more intense than that displayed by the whole Mesopotamian Force for a beloved commander. He was a great leader, and his men could ill spare one whose "confident smile had been an assurance that no sacrifice he demanded of them would be in vain."

A young officer serving in his army voiced their feelings when he wrote—

> "'Thou art a living purpose, being dead,
> Fruitful of nobleness in lesser lives,
> A guardian and a guide: Hail and farewell!'"

His men would carry on.

22. THE WESTERN FRONT— VERDUN, SOMME

"There's but one task for all,
For each one life to give,
Who stands if Freedom fall?
Who dies if England live?"
—R. KIPLING (FOR ALL WE HAVE AND ARE).

During 1915 the Allies had made various attempts to break through on the Western Front, but without success. The Germans, on the other hand, had discovered methods of using their masses of artillery, which had resulted in a great breakthrough in Galicia, and a completely successful campaign.

The German Higher Command, therefore, decided to turn their attention during 1916 to the Western Front, and to employ the same methods which had proved so successful against the Russians. They planned to deliver their attack early in the year before the Allies could prepare a spring offensive, and the place they chose was Verdun. The reason they chose Verdun was because it was situated at the point of a bulge in the line, and could be attacked from three sides at once, as the map will show. Having decided on the place, the Germans proceeded to mass an amazing quantity of guns of all sizes in the neighbourhood, which they managed to do with comparative secrecy, partly owing to the superiority in the air, which they held at that time, and partly because the country, with its evergreen fir-wooded heights, lent itself admirably to concealment.

The leadership of the enterprise was entrusted to the German

Crown Prince, in order to give it prestige, and picked troops were assembled under his command. At the beginning of the battle the Germans had seven army corps assembled against the two army corps of the French defenders.

At dawn on 21st February the great bombardment began. Grand masses of heavy guns concentrated their fire on short lengths of the French trenches, and literally obliterated them. Then, when this hurricane of explosives was moved on to another point, thousands of light field guns maintained an unending curtain of fire on the communication trenches behind, so that no reinforcements could come up.

The German infantry did not then storm forward in waves to take the shattered lines, as had previously been done by both sides, but patrols came cautiously forward to discover if it was safe for the main body of troops to advance. In this way the Germans hoped to hammer their way through by weight of metal alone, saving the valuable lives of their infantry, and only using them to protect their gunners while the latter were moving forward the guns.

But they had reckoned without the French, who foiled their plan. They withdrew practically all their men from the front line, so that a great percentage of that tremendous storm of metal expended itself in the earth in vain: they then came out of their shelters, and caught and annihilated the patrols. Then the masses of grey-clad Germans were forced to come on and meet them face to face—and often hand to hand, and in spite of the odds against them, the spirit of Verdun enabled the French to hold them at bay. This desperate resolve to oppose the Germans to the last was the main defence of Verdun. That deathless cry "Ils ne passeront pas!" which became the battle cry of France, was the outward manifestation of a spirit which could not be broken.

On Friday, 26th February, the Kaiser himself arrived to see the capture of the Douanmont plateau, the key to the whole position: the German and neutral papers had been filled with anticipation of the fall of Verdun, and a special train containing neutral journalists had been brought to Etain, so that they might proceed to the plateau next day, and proclaim the prowess of German arms to the world. Then at the last moment, the Breton Army Corps, hastily brought to Verdun, delivered a brilliant counter-attack, and not only saved the situation, but, pushing the enemy back more than a mile, so entrapped him that he could not extricate himself in this area. From this moment Verdun became more than a military objective—its moral and political importance predominated. To France it had become the very heart of her defence: to Germany the emblem of thwarted ambition. The Kaiser had boasted and promised Verdun to his people, and it is alleged that his estimate of its worth was 200,000 German casualties.

The German plan had broken down, but, in spite of the terrible daily loss of life, they were now committed to a desperate venture for which nothing but ultimate success would atone. Meanwhile the Allies were now certain that Verdun was the only German objective at the moment, and reinforcements were being hurried there by every line and road. From this time onward the defence was practically assured, but for the sake of prestige and the moral of the people at home, the Germans became more and more involved in operations wherein enormous numbers of men were sacrificed. The battles and counter-battles, which raged round Verdun, each one forming an epic in itself, continued until the last week in June, when the British and French offensive on the Somme was launched. In this mad holocaust, continued beyond all limits of common-sense, in order to try and save the name of the Emperor and his son, nearly half a million Germans became casualties, out of the million who were brought into action there.

> "Three hundred thousand men, but not enough
> To break this township on a winding stream.
> More yet must fall, and more, 'ere the red stuff
> That built a nation's manhood may redeem
> The Master's hopes, and realise his dream.
>
> "They pave the way to Verdun; on their dust
> The Hohenzollern mount, and, hand in hand,
> Gaze haggard south: for yet another thrust
> And higher hills must heap, 'ere they may stand
> To feed their eyes upon the promised land."

While this titanic struggle had been going on during the first half of the year, the new British armies had been gathering in France, and learning their work in comparatively quiet portions of the line, until by the end of June they were considered ready to take the offensive. The ground chosen was on both sides of the Somme, the British on the north, the French on the south. The Allies had the greatest confidence that they would be able to break through on a large scale, partly because of the abundance of guns and material which they had collected, and partly because they possessed a greater superiority in numbers than they had had hitherto.

The battle was heralded by a tremendous bombardment along the whole front from 24th June to 1st July, on which day the troops got out of their trenches, and advanced. The French met with a certain amount of success, probably because the Germans had not considered them capable of making an attack so soon after the terrible toll of Verdun. The British, however, met with much stiffer resistance, and although they gained a certain amount of ground, the first day's fighting cost them 50,000 casualties. Such losses as these were prohibitive, and it was obvious that the attack could not continue on this scale. The tactics had to be changed, and from this moment the battle of the Somme became a series of local attacks, nibbling away at the German defences. The new British troops, together with the South African forces, fought magnificently, and continued to make small gains of ground almost daily, but at a terrible cost in human lives. These gains, however, were sufficient to maintain the confidence of the British people for some time, and there was always the hope and expectation that the breaking-point of the Germans would be reached.

Perhaps it was not fully realised at the time that a great change had taken place in the German direction of the war on the Western Front. On 29th August, Hindenburg, with Ludendorff as his right-hand man, had become Chief of the Staff in place of Falkenhayn, who had been removed after his costly failure at Verdun. These two men were the great military geniuses of the war, and they were the first to realise how best to modify the principles of war to suit modern conditions. Their new system of defence proved as successful as their new methods of attack had proved in Galicia in 1915, and the battle of the Somme continued without any decisive success until the middle of November, when it died away in rain and mud.

One feature of this battle was the first introduction of the tank. The tanks had been manufactured with the greatest secrecy, and there is no doubt that they came as a complete surprise to the Germans, and exercised a great moral effect. Unfortunately there were not enough of them, and no definite plan for their use had been made, nor any arrangements for taking advantage of the terror and consternation of the enemy when first they appeared. The surprise was gone, and no vital result had been obtained. It was the same when the Germans first used their gas at Ypres. Surprise is invaluable, but it must be exploited to the full at once: the enemy must not be given time to recover from it.

The battle of the Somme certainly relieved the pressure at Verdun, and enabled the French to regain nearly all the ground which they had lost: a certain amount of ground had been taken, but there was left an unbroken German battle line. Perhaps the greatest result of this battle was that it proved that the new British armies and Dominion troops were the equal of any troops in the world in heroism and powers of endurance, and this fact gave great hopes for success in the coming year.

23. THE BATTLE OF JUTLAND

"Sleep not, my country, though night is here, afar
Your children of the morning are clamorous for war.
Fire in the night, O dreams
Though she send you, as she sent you long ago
South to desert, east to ocean, west to snow,
West of these, out to seas colder than the Hebrides I must go,
Where the fleet of stars is anchored and the young
Star Captains glow."

—Flecker (Dying Patriot).

It was now twenty-two months since the beginning of the Great War, and as yet, although there had been desperate fighting on land, the long-expected battle between the two greatest fleets in the world had not taken place. It was 111 years since Nelson had won the last great naval action with the British fleet at Trafalgar. It would be a fateful day, when British ships fought again against a worthy foe. The new German Fleet was yet untried, but known to be well organised and well commanded.

It was May 1916, and the British Grand Fleet was keeping watch over the great North Sea under Admiral Jellicoe. At Scapa Flow, by the Orkneys, the great battleships rode at anchor, while farther south, in the Firth of Forth, the battle cruisers lay under the command of Admiral Beatty.

From time to time, the great ships made thrilling secret sweeps over the North Sea waters, and it Happened at the end of May 1916 that one of these periodic sweeps had just been planned to take place. This time rumours were afloat of a hungry

German Fleet thirsting for action. It was not unnatural. The general military situation was not satisfactory for Germany just now. On the Western Front, Verdun had been a failure, and Russia was still giving trouble. A successful naval demonstration would hearten up the whole German nation!

So the German High Seas Fleet left its harbours and steamed out into the North Sea, part under Admiral von Hipper and part under Admiral von Sheer.

The afternoon of Tuesday, 30th May, was one of almost summer warmth, with clear skies ashore and a dead calm at sea, when Admiral Jellicoe, on board his flagship the *Iron Duke*, and Sir David Beatty, on board the *Lion*, each left headquarters according to plan, and steamed forth into the North Sea toward the opposite coast of Jutland.

Never before in history had such a powerful array of fighting ships been grouped under one command, and manned by men steeped in traditions of England's long mastery of the seas. Here was British sea strength in all its glory.

By 2 o'clock in the early morning of 31st May, the Grand Fleet in its two divisions had reached their appointed places, some seventy-seven miles apart, and Beatty was turning north to join Admiral Jellicoe with his six battle cruisers—the "Cats," as they were called—the *Lion*, *Tiger*, *Queen Mary*, and *Princess Royal*, with the *Indefatigable* and *New Zealand*. Suddenly, across the still waters came a signal, "Enemy in sight," and every man on the battle cruisers went to his appointed station. Soon five battle cruisers under Admiral von Hipper came in sight. It seemed as if the long-expected battle was coming. It was between 3 and 4 o'clock that summer's afternoon, when the first shot from the *Lion* rang through the air.

The battle of Jutland had begun. Soon, at a range of 102 miles, both sides were pressing the attack with the utmost vigour. The German gunnery was excellent, and within a short time the great British battle cruiser *Indefatigable* was struck. She rolled over and went down, with all hands, into the merciless waters of the deep North Sea. A few minutes later the *Queen Mary* was struck. A salvo of German shells hit the quarter-deck, a terrific explosion followed, and the finest ship in the British navy went down with her human freight of 1300 men and boys.

At a speed of 30 miles an hour, firing as they raced, the great vessels in parallel lines now raced southward—von Hipper to meet the rest of the German High Seas Fleet now hurrying up to meet him, Beatty to cut him off from his base. Suddenly—it was after half-past four in the afternoon—Beatty sighted von Sheer's Battle Fleet about to join forces with von flipper. He was now in face of overwhelming odds, two of his best ships gone. He did not hesitate. He knew, what the German commanders did not know, that Admiral Jellicoe was some fifty miles to the north with the main British Fleet, and he hoped as he quickly turned north to draw the whole German Fleet after him to do battle.

Again the two fleets raced in parallel lines, some eight miles apart, firing as they went. The weather was now changing for the worse, and as evening grew on, mist hid many of the enemy's ships. It was nearly 6 o'clock when, in a drift of smoke and sea haze, the British Fleet hove into sight.

Soon the greatest naval action of modem times was in full swing between the mightiest ships in the world. The noise was terrific. "Sheets of fire issued forth amid clouds of smoke." It was difficult to realise what was happening—so vast was the range, so confusing the numbers of ships engaged. It would be impossible to record all the heroism displayed in the midst of the battle, but, as typical of many, the marvelous bravery of the boy John Cornwall on board H.M.S. *Chester* stands forth. It is recorded in the Commander-in-Chief's Report of the Jutland Bank Battle as a splendid instance of devotion to duty.

"Boy (First-class) John Travers Cornwall of *Chester* was mortally wounded early in the action. He nevertheless remained standing alone in a most exposed post, quietly awaiting orders till the end of the action, with the gun's crew dead and wounded all around him. His age was under 16 ½ years. I regret that he has since died, but I recommend his case for special recognition in justice to his memory, and as an acknowledgment of the high example set by him." His well-earned V.C. was presented to his mother.

It was about half-past six when Admiral Hood's Flagship the *Invincible* was sunk, and with her perished one "who in faithfulness and courage must rank with the nobler figures of British naval history." Night was coming on. Searchlights played through the mist, and phantom ships appeared and disappeared in the gloom.

But the situation had become very serious by this time for the German High Sea Fleet, when Admiral Sheer adopted the desperate remedy of turning all his ships away from the British line. It was a movement of great risk. But under cover of a dense artificial fog produced by German destroyers, it was successfully accomplished, and soon contact between the Fleets was lost. By 9 o'clock the German Fleet had completely disappeared, and darkness made it necessary for the British admirals to ensure the safety of their ships for the night and renew fighting with dawn.

During that "uneasy darkness" the Germans made good their escape; so that when the sun rose through heavy mists next morning, nothing was to be seen of the enemy. Four hundred miles from his base, though in unchallenged possession of the field, Admiral Jellicoe now sailed for home waters.

Meanwhile the German commander, overjoyed at having escaped destruction, had already proclaimed a great German victory! The Kaiser had at once visited his broken Fleet at Wilhelmshaven, and by wireless and by telephone the news of a great British naval disaster found its way throughout the world.

"The gigantic Fleet of England, ruler of the seas," ran his words, "which since Trafalgar for a hundred years has imposed on the whole world a bond of sea tyranny, came into the field. That gigantic Armada approached, and our Fleet engaged it. The British Fleet is beaten. British world supremacy has disappeared." But though the toll of victory was great, the British Fleet still rode supreme on the waters of the North Sea, while the German ships had retired to the shelter of their harbours, where they remained until the end of the War.

News of the victory was received with enthusiasm throughout the Empire.

"The men were splendid," was the simple comment of a naval officer.

"The officers were magnificent," was the quick response of the sailors.

> "Admirals all, for England's sake
> Honour be yours and fame!
> And honour as long as the waves shall break
> To Nelson's peerless name."

The greatest naval battle in modern history was to be followed, a few days later, by the news of a sea tragedy that carried Lord Kitchener, the maker of the new armies now fighting on the Western Front, to his death.

For nearly two years the Commander-in-Chief of the new armies had worked untiringly and ungrudgingly for his country. He had thus raised the United Kingdom to the status of a great military power, and to some it had seemed as if his work might be almost done.

But our ally Russia was badly in need of arms and munitions, and it was decided that Lord Kitchener should now visit Russia and examine thoroughly the whole Russian situation, which even now was causing her Allies deep anxiety. The *Hampshire*, just returned with the Fleet after the battle of Jutland, was put at his disposal, and he arrived at Thurso on the morning of 5th June 1916. With his staff, he crossed at once on a destroyer to visit Admiral Jellicoe on board his flagship the *Iron Duke* before setting sail for Archangel, *en route* for Russia.

A heavy north-easterly gale was blowing, and a wild rough sea was dashing around Scapa Flow. Later in the day, he bade farewell to the Admiral, and embarked on board the *Hampshire*. At 5 P.M. that afternoon the ship sailed to her doom.

> "Wild were the headland skerries,
> And wilder the sunset's frown,
> And the kelpie lords were abroad in the dark,
> When Kitchener went down."

The *Hampshire* was accompanied by two destroyers, but so violent grew the gale and so high the waves that the captain ordered them to return. Then, suddenly the *Hampshire* struck a mine, only 12 miles from shore, and sank in a few minutes. In the bitter waters and with heavy seas running, the strongest swimmer had little chance, and only a few survived.

When daylight dawned, it became known that the man who

had served his country so faithfully in the great emergency had gone down with the captain and crew on the *Hampshire*.

> "Thy work was done
> Ere we could thank thee;
> and the high sea swell
> Surgeth unheeding where thy proud ship fell
> By the lone Orkneys, at the set of sun."
> —(R. Bridges on Lord Kitchener.)

24. ITALY JOINS THE ALLIES

"Blessed are those who will return with Victory, for they shall behold the Vision of a new Rome, the brow of Dante crowned afresh, the beauty of triumphant Italy."

—D'ANNUNZIO, 1915.

In November 1914 Turkey had joined with Germany and Austria in the Great War. Six months later Italy threw in her lot with the Allies—Great Britain, France, Russia, and Belgium. As a member of the Triple Alliance she had remained neutral when her two fellow-members—Germany and Austria—went to war, and Baron Sonnino, one of the most remarkable figures in the public life of Europe for thirty years the ruler and guide of Italian politics—was a stout champion of the Triple Alliance, and a stern advocate of neutrality. Now, accusing Austria of breaking the terms of the Alliance by her invasion of Serbia, he demanded a price for a continuance of neutrality.

"What price are you prepared to offer for this breach of the Triple Alliance?" asked Sonnino, while Italy quietly put her army on a war basis.

"The Trentino and Trieste," demanded the Italian leader.

Austria refused, and Great Britain stepped in with a higher price for Italy's allegiance. In return for her help the Allies offered not only the Trentino and Trieste, but all Dalmatia and most of the Adriatic Islands.

On 26th April a Treaty was signed by the Allies, and a few days later Sonnirio tore up the Triple Alliance.

On 7th May the *Lusitania*, a passenger ship, was torpedoed

by Germans in the Atlantic. Over 1000 were drowned, including women and children. The incident roused Italy's wrath, but still the Italians wavered.

The hour produced the man—neither a prince nor politician, but a poet. Gabriele D'Annunzio, Italian poet and writer, suddenly came on the scene, and lifted up his voice. On 4th May 1915, he arrived at Genoa and made the first of his impassioned speeches, putting into words the vague thoughts that were stirring in many minds, until Italian hearts beat with a new resolve, and Italian minds shone with a clear purpose.

His faith in the great destiny of Italy infected his vast audience: "He set the trumpet to his lips and blew; and the note rang high and thrilling through the mists that still drifted about the airs of Italy."

"Listen, listen," he cried. "The fatherland is in danger, and is on the road to destruction. In order to save her from ruin and ignominy it is the duty of every one of us to devote himself utterly and to arm himself with every weapon. Every good citizen must fight without respite or quarter."

From Genoa he passed to Rome. The atmosphere was electric. Peace or war hung in the balance. For seven nights the orator poured forth his "torrents of impassioned prose" to the listening Romans. He recalled to them the glories of their past history, the deeds of those who had fought for Italian freedom.

The time had arrived for Italy to come into line with the great modern nations. No longer should she be looked on as a "museum, an inn, a pleasure resort, under a sky painted with Prussian blue."

"They think us powerless—we who are the inheritors of Rome; they hold us idle and weak —we whose labouring hands have built the railways and harbours of the world; they think us changeful, though we have held fast to the ideal of a Greater Italy, which now we shall live to see fulfilled."

On 23rd May 1915, amid outbursts of popular enthusiasm, Italy declared war on Austria-Hungary. Rome was wild with joy. The King, Victor Emmanuel, with his young son beside him, the tricolour in his hand, was warmly cheered. The Italian army was highly organised, though the Germans might ridicule it as an army of "mandoline players, beggars, and brigands," and prophesy that they would soon run howling away before the conquering armies of the Austrian Emperor, Francis Joseph.

All her military efforts were concentrated on securing those most cherished places—the Trentino and Trieste. The land known as the Trentino runs down like a wedge into Italian territory. From the plains Italy looked up to Italian mountains in the hands of Austria; Austrian fortresses frowned down over her richest provinces. Thus along the northern frontier, the Italians had to fight uphill, while the enemy could hold the heights with inferior troops.

But the Alpini, the finest mountain troops in the world, were soon at work in the Trentino, and soon secured good positions along the great 300-mile frontier of high Alps. Indeed their capture of the great Alpine giant, Monte Nero, which towers above Caporetto, in June 1915, was one of the finest feats in the whole war. From here the mountains are lower, for the river Isonzo plunges southward into a deep gorge, flowing out by Monte Sabotino to the city of Gorizia, the key of Trieste. This was to be the scene of the fiercest of Italy's fighting.

Here, then, behind the Isonzo river, the Austrians were gathered in strength, safe beneath the heights of Monte Sabotino, which was strongly defended. They held it for a year against fierce attacks, in which hundreds and thousands of Italians laid down their lives. In the spring of 1916 the Italians prepared their great attack on Gorizia, the conquest of which should open the road to Trieste.

At dawn on Sunday, 6th August 1916, a deafening bombardment was opened by the Italians—louder and more terrific than had ever been heard before—against the Austrian front, and by early afternoon the heights of Monte Sabotino had been won by the Italians. The great mountain, which had defied Italy for fifteen months, had been captured in a few hours. The defenders, who had lived in deep caverns on the mountain-side, had been caught like mice in a trap, and they were now hurried down as prisoners. Three more days of fierce fighting for Gorizia, and the Italian troops entered as conquerors in triumph. The beaten Austrian army retreated hastily to positions on the Carso upland, leaving 19,000 prisoners and quantities of heavy guns, rifles, and cartridges.

The battle had opened the gate to Trieste, but the Italians had yet before them the waterless and trackless Carso country, which was yet to cost them dear.

On 21st November 1916 the Emperor of Austria, Francis Joseph, the oldest sovereign in the world, died in his eighty-sixth year after a reign of sixty-eight years. "An old man, broken with the storms of State," he had "gravely misruled the peoples entrusted to his care." Some pity may be felt for his tragic career, but otherwise he was but little missed from a land which he left ruined and bankrupt.

His successor was the Archduke Charles, nephew of the murdered heir Francis Ferdinand.

All through the winter of 1916 fighting continued. The Austrian army was then stiffened by Germans, and attacks on a large scale were planned which should bring Italy to her knees.

General Mackensen, after his victories over Russia, was now brought to conduct the new offensive.

In October 1917 the Austro-German armies were ready, and terrific fighting took place along the banks of the Isonzo river and to the north of Gorizia. So numerous were the heavy guns fired by the enemy that the whole scene has been described as a "landscape of flashes." England had sent troops to help the Italians, but the enemy was too strong for them this time. A terrible poisoned gas, new to the Italian troops, disabled and tortured them. Rain fell heavily, and dense fogs collected along the banks of the river. Through this mist the German storming troops broke through the Italian lines. Then the city of Gorizia was pounded into ruins, and fell on 29th October into the hands of the Germans, while Italian armies were everywhere retreating.

The whole sequence of events is known to history by the word "Caporetto," after a little Alpine market town on the Isonzo river, round which the main fighting took place. After the fall of Gorizia came the terrible Italian retreat. At first it was orderly, but then, hustled by the victorious foe, a sudden feeling that all was indeed lost, infected the army. Several regiments, having been isolated, laid down their arms without a struggle; many from sheer war-weariness flung away their rifles. The roads were crowded with refugees, there was no traffic control, miserably the masses moved slowly along. Rain fell steadily, increasing the mental depression of the beaten army.

And none could tell them then that a year later they would march over the same ground to victory.

No light task remained to rally the shattered Italian armies, pushed back some twelve miles beyond their eastern frontier. England and France came to the rescue, and soon the impossible seemed to happen. The feeling of discontent passed—a new spirit of determined resolve came over the nation. Every one, from the King to the poorest peasant, realised that new lines must be formed and held against the foe.

"Here they shall not pass," became the universal cry; and perhaps nothing more wonderful happened in the whole course of the war than the great rally of Italy after the Caporetto defeat.

The movement was led by the King, Victor Emmanuel. He had been at the front since the beginning of the war, visiting trenches and exposed positions, sharing meals with the soldiers, simple in his ways, and ever respected for his courage. Sitting one day with a dying soldier who was comforting himself that he had given his life, "for you, Majesty,"—"No, no, my son," was the King's grave reply, "for Italy."

He now multiplied his efforts a thousandfold, and his proclamation of November 1917 was as a trumpet call to the whole nation. "As never My House nor My People, united in a single spirit, have ever wavered before danger," ran the words, "so, even now, we must look adversity in the face undaunted. Citizens and soldiers must be a single army."

With the Allies a strong line of defence was formed behind the river Piave, held for a year, beyond which the Austro-German army failed to move them. Fighting went on into 1918, until at the last the Italians broke through—broke as a flood rushing forward to overwhelm what once had been "the proudest army in the world." The great battle of Viturio Veneto gave the victory to Italy, and the Austrian armies fled eastward and ever eastward—away from the land of Italy. They left 600,000 prisoners and 7000 machine-guns—the largest haul of the whole war. The way to Trentino and Trieste was now open, and an armistice was signed on 4th November 1918 between Italy and Austria, by which all territory allotted by the Treaty of London was to be restored.

25. THE LAST EFFORTS OF RUSSIA

"Something is rotten in the state of Denmark."
—Hamlet.

Although the year 1915 opened brightly for Russia, the great cloud which was soon to engulf her was already beginning to spread over the land. The stalemate was over, and the great fortress of Przemysl—the stronghold of Galicia,—besieged by them since September, fell into the hands of the Russians. Immense joy spread over the country, for had not the fortress been declared impregnable? The Tsar hurried to take possession of his new conquest. He drove through the conquered city of Lemberg, and on his return he sent a sword with a handle set in diamonds, inscribed: "To the conqueror of Galicia"—the Grand Duke Nicholas.

Two months later Galicia was reconquered by the Austrians. The Russian Army, short of munitions from the beginning, was now in desperate need of supply. Indeed many of the soldiers were armed only with sticks. Boots and clothing were also quite inadequate.

"The army cannot go on fighting without rifles or boots," pleaded their officers. "Without arms we must surrender all that we have won."

Such, then, was their unhappy condition, when a great offensive was begun by united German and Austrian forces under General Mackensen and the Archduke Franz Ferdinand. They chose Galicia for their attack, and by May they had driven the ill-equipped Russians towards Przemysl.

With an overwhelming supply of heavy guns they bombarded the stronghold. Stubbornly, heroically the Russians fought, but they were unequal to the task. The fortress fell into German hands. Three weeks later Lemberg was restored to the Austrians, and the Russians were in full retreat. Soon the conquest of Galicia was complete, and the great victorious armies of Germany and Austria turned to the invasion of Poland. Enormous forces of Russians guarded the main line of the railway from Warsaw to Petrograd, and soon it was known that the city—the capital of Poland and one of the most precious gems in the Russian Crown—was in danger. Even now great armies were advancing, and the Russians were not in a fit state to defend it.

It was 15th July when the Grand Duke Nicholas decided that he could not stay, and further retreat was necessary. He knew but too well the terrible impression the evacuation was bound to produce at home, but he was powerless. The garrison, hospitals, post-offices, banks were all withdrawn, and Warsaw was isolated from the outside world before the Russians left.

Then on 4th August the news spread that Warsaw had been entered by a German Prince at the head of a German Army, and the Russians were everywhere in retreat. A fortnight later Kovno, a great Russian fortress, fell into the enemy's hands with immense quantities of war material, which were now being accumulated there. It was not till October 1915 that the Russian retreat ended, and enemy troops under Mackensen were secretly withdrawn for the invasion of Serbia. A deep impression had been created throughout Russia by the retreat, and after the fall of Kovno reproaches were heaped on the Grand Duke Nicholas as Commander-in-Chief of the Armies.

The Tsar was now persuaded to remove the Grand Duke, and take over the command of his armies himself. This was the work of the so-called monk Rasputin, who had great influence over the Tsar and Tsarina at this time. The whole nation, said Rasputin, wished for their Tsar and no one else to take command of the army in the field. A month later an Imperial order told the world that the Grand Duke Nicholas had been given a command in the Caucasus. Thither an Imperial train took him from the little field station, the headquarters of the Russian army, to Tiflis. The Tsar came to wish him good-bye, and watched till the commanding figure of Nicholas, his hand raised at the salute, was carried out of sight. How well he did in his new quarters is a matter of history. He launched a sudden new offensive movement on the Caucasus front, which, directed against the Turks, led to the Russian conquest of Armenia.

Meanwhile the Tsar made a journey all along the northern front, accompanied for the first time by his young heir Alexis, the Tsarevitch, now a delicate boy of eleven, to be presented to the soldiers. Right up to Riga, the old Baltic capital, now being attacked by the Germans, they drove, even to the advanced lines held by Russian troops. Amid the deafening roar of the big guns, with Russian aeroplanes overhead, the Tsar, dressed in the grey overcoat worn by the Russian soldiers, walked along the lines with measured steps, holding his little son by the hand. The following day brought news of the successful defence of Riga. Amid scenes of great enthusiasm and the singing of the Russian national anthem, the Tsar addressed his troops. "The whole of Russia rejoices together with me and my son at your successes. I feel proud to stand at your head. Let me thank you for your heroic conduct to-day."

For the moment the Tsar of all the Russias and his young son Alexis were as popular as any monarch in Europe.

The Last Efforts of Russia

Two years later he was to be shot, with his son in his arms, by order of those who had once cheered him.

Meanwhile the spirit of Russia rose, and a grim determination to win the war characterised her every action. All through the winter 1915-16 great preparations were made for a new offensive. Fresh guns were provided, ammunition was plentiful, and the army could pour forth a very "hurricane of fire" which must win for them fresh victories. Toward the Rumanian frontier the Russians moved. By June they were ready with a well-planned offensive against Austria, which succeeded beyond all expectation. After a fortnight's hard fighting the Austrian armies were broken and retreating, while an enormous number of officers, men, and guns fell into Russian hands. An advance of fifty miles had been made—Galicia had been re-entered.

It seemed as if General Brussilov, one of the most famous of the Russian commanders, might still lead his armies to victory. German reinforcements now appeared, only to receive a "baptism of fire that had scarcely been equaled in the campaign. All the bitterness, the sufferings, with which was strewn the long path of our retreat, were poured out in this fire."

The early days of July still found the Russians pressing forward. "Nothing stayed their remorseless progress."

By August their victories were at an end. Russia's flood-mark had been reached and was never to be reached again.

The fortunes of war were still undecided when the news ran over Europe: "Rumania has entered the war on the side of Russia and the Allies."

It was the end of August 1916. King Carol, the maker of Rumania, had died early in the war of a broken heart. Once an officer in the Prussian Guard, his sympathies had always been with Germany, and he had concluded a secret treaty with the

Central Powers without the consent of the Rumanian people. His nephew and successor Prince Ferdinand had married an English Princess, Marie, daughter of the Duke of Edinburgh, who made no secret of her sympathy with the Allies. For two years Rumania had remained neutral. Now, Russia was pressing her to enter the war and to help in Brussilov's successful advance toward Galicia.

"The Central Powers have flung the world into the melting-pot, and old treaties have disappeared along with more valuable things." War was declared, and the Rumanian army crossed the northern passes of the South Carpathians.

Disaster, not victory, crowned their efforts. That same day, 28th August, the Kaiser sent for Hindenburg. He had saved Germany at Tannenberg. He was to save her again. On 5th December 1916, Bucharest, Rumania's capital, was entered by the triumphant Germans. Rumania had collapsed.

The Kaiser himself now intervened.

"A ruler is wanted," he declared, "with a conscience, who is inspired by a desire to deliver the world from sufferings. I have the courage to do it."

In December a note was addressed to the Allies, emphasising the "indestructible strength of Germany and her Allies—Austria, Turkey, and Bulgaria.

"To-day we raise the question of peace, which is a question of humanity. If our enemies decline we can proceed on our way. We are ready for war, and we are ready for peace."

The reply of the Allies—signed by Russia, France, Great Britain, Italy, Serbia, Belgium, Montenegro, Rumania and others—was firm and decided.

"Once again the Allies declare that no peace is possible which does not guarantee the future security of the world."

It was followed by a manifesto by the Kaiser to the German army. "Our enemies have declined our suggestion. They desire the destruction of Germany. They must bear the heavy responsibility for the further terrible sacrifice which I desired to spare you."

Men remembered Great Britain's pact in the autumn of 1914. "We shall never sheathe the sword which we have not lightly drawn until Belgium and Serbia recover in full measure all and more than they have sacrificed, until France is secured against the menace of aggression, and until the military domination of Prussia is wholly and finally destroyed."

That the German peace terms included her annexation of Belgium was well known.

> "'Fight on, my men,' said Sir Andrew Barton,
> 'I am hurt, but I am not slain;
> I'll lie me down to rest awhile,
> And then I'll rise and fight again.'"

26. THE RUSSIAN REVOLUTION

"Weep, my holy Russia, weep!
For thou art entering into darkness.
Weep, my holy Russia, weep!
For thou shalt shortly die."

—Boris Goduvenov.

But if, to the world at large, the military situation in Russia was less acute, within, storm-clouds were gradually spreading through the land. Since the disasters of 1915, signs of disagreement had appeared between the Imperial Government and the people. Throughout 1916, internal affairs grew from bad to worse, and by the beginning of 1917 the relation between governor and governed was strained to breaking-point.

Nicholas II., the Tsar, was now fifty-eight, well-meaning but weak. He lacked the strength of character to carry through a war, difficult, long, and wearisome. The Tsarina, his wife, had been a German Princess on her father's side, a grand-daughter of Queen Victoria on her mother's, and was accused of being in sympathy with the land of her birth. Pro-German influences began to work at the Court, and she was said to be the centre of a party working for peace with or without victory. Both Tsar and Tsarina were also under the influence of a Siberian monk, Rasputin, who was held to possess supernatural powers. Moreover, to Rasputin was attributed the recovery of the little Tsarevitch Alexis from a dangerous illness some years before, which had raised him to high favour in Russian Court circles. His lightest word became law, and, ignorant peasant though he might be, he was consulted on high matters of State. "Few more squalid figures have ever reached supreme power in a great nation before."

This supreme influence in war and politics was bitterly resented by the Russian Duma or Parliament of the people. On 29th December 1916, Rasputin was murdered, and while the Tsar and Tsarina mourned deeply for their friend and adviser, the country applauded the deed with great joy and relief.

The death of Rasputin was the first act in the Russian Revolution. How would it all end?

The winter of 1916-17 had been exceptionally cold and dreary, with heavy falls of snow, and, amid general disorganisation, the supply of food had been scanty. Indeed by February the daily bread allowance in Petrograd was threatened with complete failure. Patiently the peasants waited for hours in the cold for bread, and long processions of helpless, hungry women begged food for their children.

The Duma discussed the vital question of food supplies, but March came in and nothing was done. Then they appealed to the Imperial Government to grapple with the problem; but nothing was done. Bread riots began, bakers' shops were looted—a crisis had been reached. People filled the streets, hungry, despairing, angry, and defiant. "The Government must go," was heard on all sides.

Petrograd was full of police, soldiers, and machine-guns. It was Sunday, 11th March, when the hungry people awoke to find a proclamation placarded over the city.

"During the last few days," it ran, "disorders have taken place in Petrograd, followed by violence. I forbid any kind of meetings in the streets. I warn the population that I have given the troops fresh orders to use their arms, and to stop at nothing to maintain order."

It was the old voice of Tsarism speaking—arrogant, unsympathetic. It was the last time it was ever to be heard. But the Government was alarmed. An urgent appeal was sent to the Tsar at Army Headquarters. "Condition serious —transport of food broken down—general discontent growing—firing proceeding in streets—delay is fatal." But all was silence. Then came a message suspending the Duma. Indignation ran high. The streets were thickly crowded. Then the Guards were ordered to fire on the mob, and the storm broke. The soldiers refused to obey. It was the revolt of human nature against an unnatural task. Mutiny was in the air. Soldiers and citizens mingled together.

"We are hungry, too," they cried. The confusion was indescribable. Amid sharp bursts of firing from the police, red flags were carried from street to street, the prisons were stormed, and criminals released. Another urgent message went to the Tsar.

"The situation is becoming worse. Measures must be taken immediately, for to-morrow it may be too late. The last hour has arrived, when the fate of the country and the dynasty is being decided."

"Can no one open the Tsar's eyes to the real situation?" they asked. "The Tsar is blind," was the despairing reply. Meanwhile the Tsar was returning to the Tsarina at Tsarskoe-Selo, when news reached him that the line to Petrograd was closed, and the Palace in the hands of the revolutionists.

"Moscow will remain faithful to me. We will go to Moscow," he replied. But Moscow, too, was in the hands of revolutionaries. The only solution was his abdication of the throne of all the Russias. "Nothing but the abdication of Your Majesty in favour of your son can still save the Russian Fatherland, and preserve the dynasty," he was told.

"I had decided to abdicate yesterday," replied the Tsar quickly, "but I cannot be separated from my son. His health is too delicate. It is more than I could bear. I shall therefore abdicate in favour of my brother Michael."

Then the Tsar signed his act of abdication. It was a memorable document.

"By the Grace of God, we, Nicholas II., Emperor of all the Russias, Tsar of Poland, Grand Duke of Finland, &c., to all our faithful subjects make known:

"In these days of terrible struggle against the foreign enemy who has been trying for three years to impose his will upon our Fatherland, God has willed that Russia should be faced with a new and formidable rival. Troubles at home threaten and have a fatal effect on the ultimate course of this hard-fought war. At this moment, a moment so decisive for the existence of Russia, our conscience bids us to facilitate the closest union of our Subjects and the organisation of all their forces for the speedy attainment of victory.

"For that reason we think it right—and the Imperial Duma shares our view—to abdicate the crown of the Russian State, and resign the supreme power.

"We appeal to all the loyal sons of Russia to do their duty at this moment of painful national crisis.

"May God help Russia!"

NICHOLAS.

Amid the general confusion reigning in Petrograd, Councils of workmen and soldiers were being formed, known as Soviets—a word meaning Council. Into their power now fell the work of guiding the Revolution. They at once refused the Grand Duke

Michael as their Tsar. "No more Romanoffs," they cried, "we want a Republic."

Meanwhile "Citizen Romanoff" and his wife were arrested for "working secretly for a restoration of the monarchy."

Snow fell heavily over the land during these critical days. The food question was still acute, and the red flag showed how matters were tending. In simple words the ex-Tsar bade farewell to his army:

"I address you for the last time, you soldiers who are so dear to my heart. May God help the new Government to lead Russia to glory and prosperity. For more than two years and a half you have continuously borne the hardships of an arduous service, and already the hour is at hand in which Russia and her glorious Allies will break down the enemy's last desperate resistance in one mighty effort. He who thinks of peace at the present moment is a traitor to Russia. May God bless you and lead you to victory."

NICHOLAS.

But there was to be no victory under the new rule. Men had grown tired of the war and only wanted peace. Everywhere there was chaos. Men at the front refused to obey orders—soldiers no longer saluted their officers. Open mutiny reigned, and by the end of July, the Russian Army as a fighting force had ceased to exist.

For the moment it seemed that a "horror of great darkness" had fallen upon the land, and that the best life-blood of the country had been shed in vain. Then two men—Lenin and Trotsky,—German in thought and action, came on the scene, and the Russian Republic fell under the rule of the Bolshevists. One of their first acts was to sue for peace, and before the unhappy year 1917 was ended, Germany was dictating hard terms of peace to Russia at Brest-Litovsk. Germany was to have Poland and other Russian provinces; she made an arrangement which placed all Russian trade and products entirely in her hands, and extorted a sum of money from her, impossible of fulfillment.

But the disgraceful Treaty was signed on 24th February 1918, and with it the Allies lost all Russia's help to the end.

The last great tragedy of the Romanoffs now drew near. For the first five months following their arrest on 21st March 1917, the ex-Tsar and his family were kept closely imprisoned in the Palace of Tsarkoe-Selo, Petrograd. They were declared traitors to their country and believed to be in league with the Germans. Even when an examination of their papers showed this to be untrue, the poisonous rumour spread. They were ill-treated and persecuted by their guards, by whom the ex-Tsar's salute was always ignored. As the weeks passed on, and the power of the people grew, the Tsar became more and more unpopular.

"When the people stretched out their hands to you, you did not meet them." These were the bitter words in which the Tsar's downfall was expressed. At last it was decided to exile the family to Siberia. Six days' hard traveling brought them to Tobolsk. As Bolshevism spread over the land, so the sufferings of the ex-Imperial family increased. They were given starvation rations, and young Alexis fell ill again. Nicholas sawed wood in the courtyard; he wore peasant's clothes, a plain khaki shirt with the cross of St. George and his colonel's shoulder straps, till these were cut off, and the cross alone remained to symbolise his loyalty to Russia. This he still wore on the day of his murder. He taught his girls their lessons, while his wife Alexandra occupied herself with needlework and nursing her sick boy. Money was very short, and the young Princesses sold their needlework and drawings to eke out a livelihood.

As time passed, they all realised the desperate nature of their position. Pathetic letters and poems have survived the last great onslaught. Spring came and Alexis grew worse. Both his legs became paralysed and he could no longer walk. Then one day in May they were all moved again—for the last time. Evil influences were rapidly spreading over Russia. Their new prison-house was at Ekaterinburg, the capital of the Ural region and a stronghold of the Bolshevists.

"Citizen Romanoff, you may enter," was the rough welcome for the once Imperial ruler of all the Russias. Around the house was a wooden hoarding reaching to the upper windows, which were whitewashed. The lower floor was occupied by guards; the prisoners were to live upstairs. It was now 22nd May, and raining heavily. Alexis was carried up, but his sisters were made to carry their luggage from the platform to the house. Sentries were stationed both inside and outside, and machine-guns were posted at given points. The whole family were now in a trap, from which there could be no escape. There was no comfort—nothing but blank despair. The guards were coarse thinking men, who entered the prisoners' rooms at will. The poorest prison fare was provided. Alexis remained an invalid, unable to walk at all. As the weeks passed on, the whole family became overwhelmed with grief and dismay. At last the end came.

On 16th July 1917 the whole family went to bed as usual. At midnight they were awakened, and told roughly to dress and come downstairs. They dressed quickly, thinking they were going to be moved once again. The ex-Tsar carried his son downstairs in his arms; the youngest girl, Anastasia, carried his King Charles spaniel. They were all led to a basement room near the front entrance looking on to the garden. Machine-guns were posted at the door. The room was bare. Chairs were brought, and the suffering Tsarina sat down beside Alexis. Suddenly volleys rang out, and all the prisoners fell to the ground. In a few moments their sufferings were over. The ex-Tsar Nicholas, his wife Alexandra, Alexis, and their four young daughters lay dead.

"Surely the murder of the Imperial family is the most appalling crime in the whole annals of history!" said a Russian. The news leaked out slowly amid the din of the European War. The Revolution was complete. It had thrown over all creeds, all morals, and the habits of the people. Once renowned for its Christian spirit, the country gave way to barbarian cruelty and blind selfishness.

And still, like a great forest fire, Bolshevism spread over the once great nation of Russia.

27. GERMANY LOSES HER COLONIES

"And courage never to submit or yield."
—Milton.

The whole force of the British Empire was now leveled against Germany, and to the newly made South African Union was allotted the task of conquering her African Colonies.

How, late in the day, she began to look round for "places in the sun" has already been told. Other countries had acquired the best places in Africa, and Germany had rather to take what was left. Thus, when war broke out, she had two strips on the west coast known as Togoland and the Cameroons, a vast waterless desert in the south-west, and a yet larger district, twice the size of the German Empire, in the east.

Even before these colonies were taken from her, Australians and New Zealanders had hastened to Kaiser Wilhelmsland, part of New Guinea, and seized the Bismarck Archipelago, thus sweeping all German outposts from the Pacific Ocean quite early in the war. Again, she had lost her Chinese province of Kaio-Chau in 1914—a great blow. The Kaiser had lavished money on the capital, which was to be the German centre for the East. It was the "apple of his eye," and the base of his Pacific Fleet. When, on the outbreak of war, the Allies demanded the return of this province to China, the Kaiser had ordered his German garrison to hold out to the last man, and they endured a bombardment from land and sea for a month. Then the 4000 Germans were obliged to surrender, and the Kaiser's Eastern stronghold was occupied by the Allies.

Germany Loses Her Colonies

Of the African colonies, Togoland was the first to fall. Situated between British and French territories, it was invaded from both sides. The Germans retired along the railway to defend their famous wireless station at Kamina. It was one of the finest in the world, but, seeing the game was up, they destroyed it and surrendered.

The Cameroons were larger than the German Empire. Without adequate preparation, British troops entered from Nigeria, only to be driven back over the border by the Germans. With the help of gunboats on the coast, the capital, Duala, was taken, and the final conquest of the vast territory stretching from the coast to Lake Chad was in time accomplished.

The conquest of German South-West Africa was a more serious matter. The country is as large as the Transvaal and Orange Free State together, involving some 300,000 square miles of barren and waterless rocky land, to defend which a stubborn defence was made. Along the thousand miles of "storm-beaten inhospitable coast," there were but two harbours, one of which, Walfisch Bay, was British. At the other harbour, with its open and wind-swept roadstead at Swakopmund, the Germans had built, on a foundation of deep and shifting sand, two well-constructed towns, from which they had run a railway into the interior to the capital, Windhok, where the most powerful long-range wireless station in the world had been constructed, with 300 feet high masts and mile long aerials, capable of talking direct to Berlin.

It is known now that, in the event of war, German West Africa was designed to be a base for an attack on British Dominions. Great masses of war material were found—guns, rifles, and ammunition, and a secret poison gas factory all told the same tale.

"Yes," said the Germans, "we expected India to rise; we expected trouble in Ireland; we expected a triumphant rebellion in South Africa; we anticipated that the British Empire would be torn in pieces."

Had it not been for General Botha's prompt and brilliant exploits in quelling the rebellion which broke out in the Transvaal on the eve of the expedition to South-West Africa, the Germans might well have been right after all. But it delayed matters seriously. Another unexpected delay came, too, in November 1914, when Admiral Cradock's squadron was sunk by the German admiral, Von Spee, off the coast of Coronel. Might not the victorious German admiral make his way to the defence of German West Africa? The sinking of his fleet in December put an end to any such possibility, and General Botha arrived at Walfisch Bay early in February 1915 in supreme command of his Union troops, well-equipped and enthusiastic, and struck his camp at Swakopmund. Four separate forces were acting in the campaign, which was brilliantly organised by General Botha, and carried out without a hitch by his loyal officers. In all, the total number of troops was about 40,000 men—far exceeding the Germans, who numbered about 9000 and who were very fully equipped with heavy guns and prepared positions. Swakopmund had been hastily evacuated by the Germans, who left behind, among other things, a gramophone in one of their larger houses, with records marked "English lessons," consisting of a series of English sentences, from which Germans could acquire some slight knowledge of English!

The other three forces were already making their way into the country "according to plan," when, toward the end of April, General Botha began his advance, the mounted men leading the way along the dry bed of the Swakopmund river, and the infantry following through the sandy and waterless waste along the track of the railway. For rapid trekking, none could beat General

Botha, and a record-breaking march, "causing two hemispheres to talk," was now made, covering 200 miles in five days over a waterless desert land. The Germans, who had boasted that the way to the capital was strewn with mines and that all water was poisoned, were surprised, and when General Botha moved in force on Karibil he found the foe in full retreat. They had left their wives and children at the mercy of the conquerors. Perfect order and confidence prevailed as the General hoisted the Union Jack over Karibil. After an arrangement with the Germans over the telephone, General Botha and his staff left Karibil, and received the surrender of 3000 Germans at Windhok, the capital of the province. The Germans had been taken by surprise, and they had barely time to destroy the famous wireless station before fleeing from that picturesque German town in the very heart of Africa to take up their last stand in the north. But round about Otavi the other forces were concentrating, and soon the Germans, cut off from their base and surrounded, were obliged to surrender.

On 9th July 1915 they laid down their arms. The conquest of their land had been completed in six months with but few casualties, and the Peace Conference handed over the "South-West Territory," as it was afterwards called, to be administered as a part of the South African Union, under a mandate from the League of Nations.

But there still remained the last and most valuable of the overseas colonies. German East Africa was twice the size of Germany herself, with some 8,000,000 natives and 5000 Europeans. She had a coast-line on the Indian Ocean of 470 miles, while her western frontier from Lake Victoria to Lake Nyasa was some 700 miles in length.

It was a magnificent country of unrivalled scenery, with its great mountain ranges and huge plains, its primeval forests, pathless and trackless, its rich black soil turning to mud in the rainy season and dust in the drought, with fierce tropical heat and the deadly tsetse-fly. It was the land of the big-game hunter, with its wild beasts and impenetrable jungle, rather than a land for military expeditions. All attempts to invade the country during the early part of the war had met with disastrous failure.

In her commander, von Lettow-Vorbeck, Germany had a brilliant man, courageous, determined, and courteous. He knew his country well, and the Kaiser had ordered him to hold out to the last—a command he obeyed loyally by being still at large when peace came in 1918.

It was not till 1916 that the South African Union was ready to co-operate in conquering this last colony, and that General Smuts arrived at Mombasa as Commander-in-Chief in charge of the campaign. He was faced with the tremendous task of driving the Germans across the frontier and rounding them up in a vast area, and this must be done before the rainy season set in and the country became a vast swamp. He had taken part in the campaign for conquering South-West Africa, and now followed somewhat the same plan so successfully carried out by his friend and comrade, General Botha. The colony was to be invaded from four quarters—two small Belgian forces from the Congo, a British force from Rhodesia, and the largest force, numbering some 20,000 men, from the Union under General Smuts himself.

On 5th March the movement began in the north of the Colony, south of the line of the famous British railway from Mombasa to Myanda, on which stood Nairobi, the capital of British East Africa, known as Kenya Colony.

The rainy season was soon due, and there was no time to be

lost. General Smuts knew, too, that the enemy must be taken by surprise, so "he adopted a plan which Lettow-Vorbeck had not dreamed of, and flung himself into the wilds." With the help of his skilful officers he entirely succeeded, and in little more than a fortnight the great mountain of Kilimanjaro, whose highest peak had been named after the Kaiser, had been conquered, and headquarters secured at Moschi, the terminus of the Tanya railway, while the enemy retreated south. The Germans had lost the richest part of their country with its vast plantations of coffee, while the loss of Kilimanjaro, the most beautiful of solitary peaks, brought home to the native army the reality of their defeat.

An invasion of the interior was now directed against the German railway running from the shores of Lake Tanganyika to the seaport capital of Dar-es-Salaam. A start was made on 3rd April. The rains now began, and progress was difficult. Horses became exhausted, armoured cars stuck in the swollen fords, but magnificently the men made their way. On the 17th the main enemy's position was attacked and carried by the weary but not disheartened troops. Cooking now grew impossible by reason of incessant rain; men had to live on short rations. Toward the end of July the railway was cut, and 100 miles of line fell into the hands of the invaders, though every bridge had been destroyed by the retreating foe. By 3rd September the capital Dar-es-Salaam was occupied by General Smuts and his victorious troops, and the conquest of German East Africa practically achieved. True, the southern part of the colony yet remained in the hands of the brilliant and resourceful Commander Lettow-Vorbeck, who, knowing his country and his men, had made such a gallant stand, but there was now no doubt as to the result.

Before the end General Smuts was called back to England

to take part in the Imperial War Conference. To him belonged the chief credit of the campaign. "He inspired his whole command with his own magnetic spirit, and lifted it over hard places, which might well have proved unconquerable without such leadership." It has been said that his was one of the most remarkable campaigns of the whole world war. His own words give a graphic picture of the hardship and suffering of the men:

"Their work has been done under tropical conditions which not only produce bodily weariness and unfitness, but which create mental depression and, finally, appall the stoutest hearts. To march day by day, through the African jungle or high grass in which vision is limited to a few yards, in which danger lurks near, supplies a test to human nature often in the long-run beyond the limit of human endurance."

28. AMERICA DECLARES WAR

"Bear witness, Earth, we have made our
choice With Freedom's Brotherhood!"
—RUDYARD KIPLING *(ON AMERICA*, 1917).

"America declares War!"

This was the news flashed into every corner of the world on that fateful day, 6th April 1917. The story of how the great Western States turned from their firm attitude of peace and neutrality during the first three years of the war to that of co-operation on a gigantic scale is one of thrilling interest.

The man who upheld the peace for the first years, and finally led America into war, was President Woodrow Wilson. His representative in England was Walter Page, American Ambassador; England's representative in America was Cecil Spring-Rice, English Ambassador. "Steadfast as any soldier of the line," these men served through the strain of those three awful years of war. Both lived to know that America had "come in"; both died before the declaration of peace.

When the Great War broke out in 1914, America had at once declared for neutrality.

"Our first and fundamental maxim should be never to entangle ourselves in the broils of Europe," declared the President, who had entered the White House little over a year before. He had dedicated his life to the preservation of peace and a program of social reform. It was not till the spring of 1915 that Germany began her submarine warfare to prevent ships entering or leaving

British waters, and torpedoing those that had already succeeded. Hundreds of British ships were thus destroyed off the coast of England and Ireland.

But on 7th May 1915, at two o'clock in the afternoon, a Cunard liner, the *Lusitania*, was struck by torpedoes fired from a German submarine. She heeled over and sank with her freight of 2000 passengers, over a thousand being drowned—men, women, and children. More than a hundred of those who were drowned were American subjects. It seemed like a deliberate attack on non-fighting travelers, citizens of a neutral State, and a wave of bitter anti-German feeling swept over America.

To the mind of the American Ambassador in England, Page, and Colonel House, the President's adviser, an impossible situation had been created. "We shall be at war with Germany within a month," declared Colonel House.

But America made no signs of yielding to the popular outcry. The President spoke of the healing influences of peace and his firm opposition to force.

Germany promised America not to torpedo another liner without warning.

On 19th August, the White Star liner *Arabic* was torpedoed without warning, and again American subjects lost their lives. Still the President satisfied himself by trying to extort pledges from Germany with regard to the ships, and on 1st September Germany gave a definite pledge: "Liners will not be sunk by our submarines without warning."

For the moment it seemed as if diplomacy and resolution might yet take the place of force. But within a few days of the pledge more ships were torpedoed, more American lives lost.

This time the President seemed stirred. "Germany," he told his country, "has broken a solemn pledge, and American patience is sorely tried. Unless Germany will abandon her present methods of warfare against passenger ships, America must sever all diplomatic relations with her. Submarine warfare is inhuman, and the only excuse America can ever have for the use of physical force is that she uses it in the interests of humanity."

Page, from the other side of the Atlantic, knew the worth of the German promise, and he warned the President again and again that America was losing prestige in Europe by her isolation policy of non-interference. It seemed as if the President grew more and more determined not to fight.

"An early peace is all that can prevent Germany from driving us at last into war," he said.

He pleaded before the "League to enforce Peace" at Washington for co-operation, instead of conflict with other nations, as a basis of permanent peace. He stood forth as a would-be mediator in the World War, rather than a fighter, and when in 1916 Germany sought to negotiate peace terms based on her conquests, another peace note was framed by the President and sent to the fighting Powers, only to be firmly refused by all.

"Nobody in Washington understands the War," explained Page. "In England there can be no peace till the German military despotism is broken."

Hurrying across to America to explain the whole situation, Page found the President out of touch with the entire world at war, absorbed only in the one idea of peace that should end war. The two old friends parted, never to meet again.

But a change came with the New Year. Early in 1917, Germany informed America that she was about to resume unrestricted submarine warfare. The President hesitated no longer. On 3rd February 1917, he announced that this act meant severing diplomatic relations with Germany. The war spirit was again sweeping over the land; Germany seemed utterly reckless. In the next few weeks American ships were torpedoed, American lives lost. At last Germany had roused the United States to fever heat. The country was ready for the final step. The long patient years of neutrality were over. With March came the Russian Revolution—England's ally had failed her. German troops set free were rushing to the Western Front. England looked across the Atlantic for help. And this time America did not fail.

The President's famous message to Congress stated the American case against Germany, of popular government against tyranny, of civilisation against barbarism.

"Ships of every kind, whatever their flag, their cargo, their destination, have been ruthlessly sent to the bottom without warning, without thought of help or mercy for those on board—even hospital ships have been sunk with the same reckless lack of pity or of principle. This warfare is a challenge to all mankind. The wrongs against which we now array ourselves cut to the very roots of human life. Our object is to uphold the principles of peace and justice in the life of the world as against selfish and autocratic power.... The world must be made safe for democracy. The right is more precious than peace, and we shall fight for the things which we have carried nearest our hearts, for the rights and liberties of small nations, for a universal dominion of right and a union of the peoples as shall bring peace and safety to all nations, and make the world itself at last free. To such a task of peace and liberation we can dedicate our lives and our fortunes, all that we are and all that we have, with the pride of those who know that the day has come, when America is privileged to spend her blood and her might for the principles that gave her birth and happiness, and the peace which she has treasured.

"God helping her, she can do no other."

The message was received with stormy enthusiasm by the audience, and a "thrill of assent ran through the length and breadth of the land." America had joined the Allies at last.

"And we are one with them—we rise With dawning thunder in our eyes, To join the embattled hosts that kept Their pact with freedom while we slept."

When the great news reached London, America's Ambassador, Page, went to break the glad tidings to the Prime Minister, Lloyd George. So great was the relief after the years of anguish and strain that he could but hold out his two hands in silence, with tears in his eyes.

Seven months later he died—the "friend of Britain in her sorest need." Hardly less strenuous had been the life of the English Ambassador in Washington. He, too, died in 1918. On his last night in office, he wrote these lines:

"I vow to thee, my country—all earthly things above, Entire and whole and perfect, the service of my love The love that asks no questions; the love that stands the test, That lays upon the altar the dearest and the best; The love that never falters, the love that pays the price, The love that makes, undaunted, the final sacrifice."

America had declared war on 6th April, and all the resources of the richest nation in the world were at once put at the disposal of the Government. Arrangements were made for raising an army of 10,000,000 men and to increase the navy. Vast training camps sprang up everywhere, and dollars poured in for guns, munitions, and aeroplanes. A fleet of destroyers started at once to hunt for submarines, and by June an advance guard of troops under General Pershing marched through London on the way to France amid great outbursts of enthusiasm.

Before the year 1917 was ended, over 150,000 Americans had landed in Europe.

"Now we are pledged to win the Rights of man, Labour and justice now shall have their way."

29. THE WESTERN FRONT—ARRAS, YPRES, AND CAMBRAI

"Now all the youth of England are on fire,
And silken dalliance in the wardrobe lies:
Now thrive the armourers, and honour's thought
Reigns solely in the breast of every man."

—SHAKESPEARE *(KING HENRY V.)*

The beginning of the year 1917 found the Allies still hopeful of success on the Western Front. The French by the end of 1916 had regained nearly all the ground lost at Verdun. General Nivelle, under whose command these counter-attacks had been made, was appointed Commander-in-Chief of the French armies, and there was a general demand for an early offensive in 1917.

In England, Lloyd George had taken over control of affairs, and inspired the country with a new spirit of confidence and optimism, and, in addition, it was hoped that the ground gained during the Somme battle would provide favourable points from which to attack the Germans early in the year.

The entry of Rumania into the war on the side of the Allies had had little effect, owing to her swift destruction, beyond general disappointment. The fatal weakening of the Russians was not yet fully appreciated; in fact, it was confidently expected that they would become once more a great fighting force during the year.

Germany had, up to date, made enormous gains of territory, but had failed to win a decisive victory over her greater opponents. Her problem lay in the fact that her people were beginning

The Western Front—Arras, Ypres, and Cambrai

to grow impatient at the delay in securing the promised rewards of victory. The people wanted a victory, yet, at the same time, it was necessary to hold on to the gains which had been made. In order to do this, enormous forces had to be maintained on all the fighting fronts, and there were not enough reserve troops left with which to launch a large offensive. As it was not possible on land, the desired offensive was made on the sea, and took the form of unrestricted submarine warfare. It was a grave risk to take, since thereby Germany became an outlaw among nations. The immediate result was the entry of the United States of America into the War on the side of the Allies.

Germany, therefore, began the year 1917 on the Western Front with the intention of holding on to what she had gained, and hoping for the success of her pirate policy on the sea. The Allies began the year with every hope of breaking through the Western Front, and marching to Berlin.

General Nivelle had devised a new plan for overcoming the hitherto impregnable German defence, and all the available French troops were being got ready to carry it out. Meanwhile, the British were to resume their attacks from Arras to Soissons, following up the advantage which they had already gained in this area. The plan was good, but the Allies had reckoned without Hindenburg and Ludendorff. These two amazing men had entirely anticipated events, and, having decided that there was no military advantage to be gained in holding this awkward salient, had begun as early as September 1916 to construct a new line of defence from the neighbourhood of Arras to that of Rheims. This line, originally called the Siegfried line, after the hero of Wagner, and later known as the Hindenburg line, was ready when the British renewed their attacks. The German withdrawal, aided by the weather, had been very skillfully made, and it was not realised at first that resistance was being offered merely by detachments left in the old positions. As the British made considerable gains, there was great exultation, and it was thought to be the beginning of a great German retreat. But suddenly the resistance stiffened, and the attackers realised that the new positions were stronger than those which had been abandoned. A desolate area of ground had been gained, for the Germans had systematically destroyed everything before they left, even to the extent of cutting down the fruit-trees. Cambrai and St. Quentin were still unattainable, and the German line was unbroken.

The Allied plan had been dislocated at the start, but it was decided that the British should make a determined attempt to take this new position, if only to keep the enemy occupied while the French carried out their great attack. Accordingly on 9th April began the battle of Arras, which continued until May. Many heroic attacks were made between Lens and St. Quentin, and a few local successes, such as the capture of Vimy Ridge by the Canadians, were attained, but once more the casualties were too great, and the German positions remained unconquered. As soon as the battle of Arras had been developed, and strong German forces were being engaged, General Nivelle struck his blow.

On 16th April, the attack was delivered between Soissons and Rheims, and the opening success was spectacular, 17,000 prisoners and 75 guns being taken in the first three days. The French losses, however, in this second battle of the Aisne soon amounted to 100,000 men, only a small portion of ground had been gained, and the attack ceased. General Nivelle was relieved of his command, and General Petain, the defender of Verdun, took his place, with General Foch as Chief of the General Staff. The new system of defence, worked out by Hindenburg

The Western Front—Arras, Ypres, and Cambrai 169

and Ludendorff from the lessons which they had learnt on the Somme, had proved unsurmountable. Both sides relapsed into trench warfare. The Germans willingly, since they were relying on their submarine campaign; the Allies unwillingly, because they could not devise a method of breaking the German lines, without incurring casualties, which they could not possibly stand.

On 7th June, however, took place an action which stands out during this period as being perfectly planned, perfectly executed, and completely successful, although its effect was purely local. This was the capture of the Messines Ridge by the British Second Army, under General Plumer. One million pounds of high explosive were used in the mines which were blown up under the German positions. The British advanced as far as they had planned to go, and, holding on to what they had gained, materially improved the uncomfortable position of the troops in front of Ypres. This battle was the one bright spot in what was otherwise a depressing period. The strain upon the Allied armies after so many unsuccessful attacks, coupled with the disappointment of the peoples at home, were having far-reaching effects.

Russia was in collapse, the Italians were unable to make progress, and the German submarine campaign was at its height. There was no longer anything in sight which promised to win a decision against Germany on the Western Front. Meanwhile, owing to the success of the under-water pirates' campaign, the ports of Zeebrugge and Ostend, from which the submarines were setting forth, became of increasing importance. Although the Allies had for the time being given up the idea of being able to break the Western Front, they thought, quite rightly, that they were strong enough to force the Germans back at any given point.

It was decided, therefore, to make an attack in Flanders, in order to make the Germans withdraw from this strip of coast, and so ease the situation on the sea. On 31st July, the offensive was launched from Dixmude to Armentieres. This, the third battle of Ypres, saw some of the most desperate fighting of the war, for the country was very difficult, and losses heavy; but although local successes were gained right up to November, the German positions were never sufficiently threatened to cause a retreat from the Belgian coast. Special preparations had been made for landing a force from the sea, and striking the enemy in the flank, but the favourable moment for this enterprise never came.

After failing to drive the Germans back from the Belgian coast, the British made one more attack before the end of the year. This was at Cambrai, on 20th November. Hitherto, before an attack was launched, it had been necessary to bring down a heavy bombardment of artillery fire on the enemy's front line, in order to destroy the masses of barbed-wire behind which he was entrenched. This preliminary bombardment always gave the enemy warning of what was going to happen, so that he was ready when the infantry started to advance. The British made a new plan, by which it was hoped to smash the enemy's front line and his wire, without giving him any warning. This was to be done by masses of tanks, which were to be followed by the infantry. The tanks were brought up under cover of darkness and mist, the noise of their engines being drowned by aeroplanes specially used for the purpose. At early dawn the attack was made, artificial smoke being added to the mist in order to make the surprise greater.

The success was complete, and the British infantry surged forward through the German positions to a depth of five miles on a front some twelve miles long. At last a real break had been made in the line, but unfortunately there was no army at hand to take advantage of it, and widen the gap. The advance stopped where the first victorious rush had taken it, and left merely a dangerous bulge into the German lines. The Germans were not long in taking advantage of this fact, and on 30th November they attacked the southern flank, and regained nearly all the ground which they had lost. In the end the losses on both sides were about equal, and, as Ludendorff states, "The action had given valuable hints for an offensive battle in the west, if we wished to undertake one in 1918."

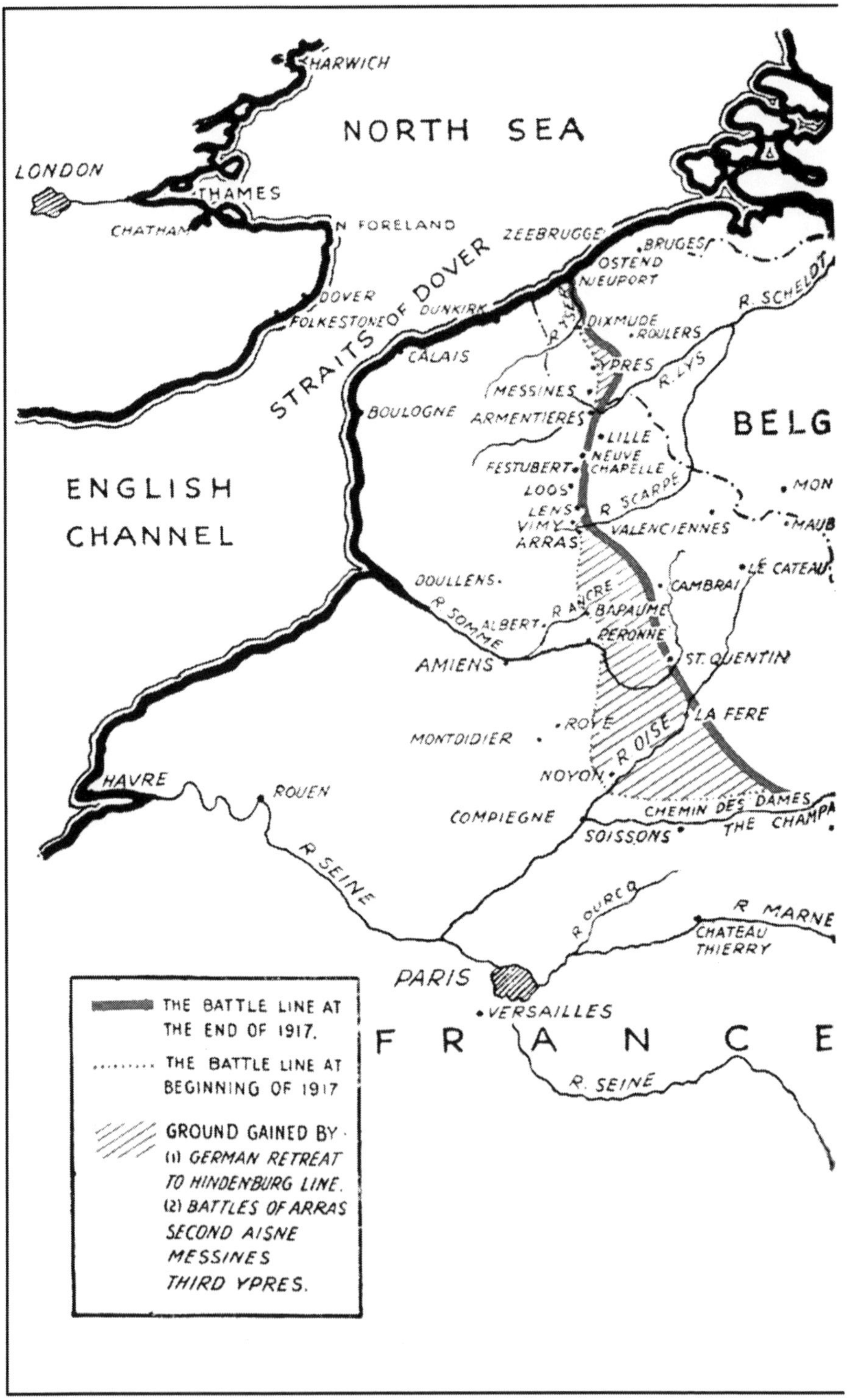
HARWICH
NORTH SEA
LONDON
THAMES
CHATHAM
N FORELAND
ZEEBRUGGE
BRUGES
OSTEND
NIEUPORT
STRAITS OF DOVER
DOVER
FOLKESTONE
DUNKIRK
DIXMUDE
ROULERS
R. SCHELDT
CALAIS
YPRES
R. LYS
MESSINES
BOULOGNE
ARMENTIERES
BELG
LILLE
NEUVE CHAPELLE
FESTUBERT
ENGLISH CHANNEL
LOOS
R. SCARPE
MON
LENS
VIMY
ARRAS
VALENCIENNES
MAUB
LE CATEAU
DOULLENS
CAMBRAI
R. ANCRE
BAPAUME
R. SOMME
ALBERT
PERONNE
AMIENS
ST. QUENTIN
LA FERE
ROYE
MONTDIDIER
R. OISE
NOYON
HAVRE
ROUEN
CHEMIN DES DAMES
COMPIEGNE
SOISSONS
THE CHAMPA
R. SEINE
R. OURCQ
R. MARNE
CHATEAU THIERRY
PARIS
VERSAILLES
FRANCE
R. SEINE
THE BATTLE LINE AT THE END OF 1917.
THE BATTLE LINE AT BEGINNING OF 1917
GROUND GAINED BY
(1) GERMAN RETREAT TO HINDENBURG LINE.
(2) BATTLES OF ARRAS
SECOND AISNE
MESSINES
THIRD YPRES.

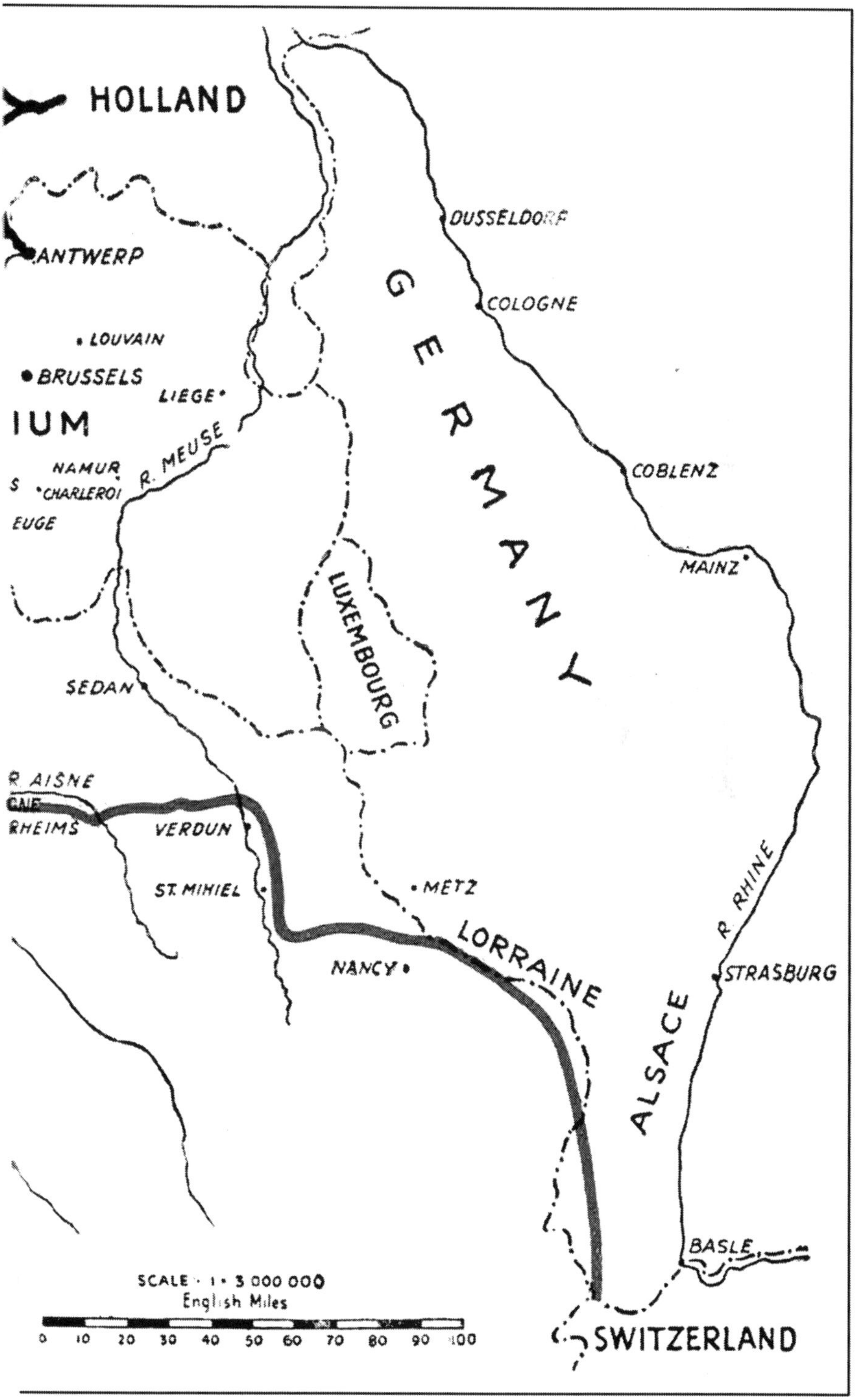

HOLLAND
ANTWERP
LOUVAIN
BRUSSELS
LIEGE
IUM
R. MEUSE
NAMUR
CHARLEROI
EUGE
DUSSELDORF
COLOGNE
GERMANY
COBLENZ
MAINZ
LUXEMBOURG
SEDAN
R. AISNE
RHEIMS
VERDUN
ST. MIHIEL
METZ
NANCY
LORRAINE
R. RHINE
STRASBURG
ALSACE
BASLE
SWITZERLAND
SCALE 1 : 3 000 000
English Miles
0 10 20 30 40 50 60 70 80 90 100

30. THE DOVER PATROL AND ZEEBRUGGE

" So age to age shall tell how they sailed through the darkness,
Where, under those high, austere, implacable
stars, Not one in ten
Might look for a dawn again."

—*Alfred Noyes* (The Vindictive).

Although America had joined the Allies in their naval attacks on the German submarines, yet in 1918 the submarine was still a very serious menace to shipping. As the years passed on, the submarines had been vastly improved—they were much faster, and their torpedoes could be fired a much greater distance than heretofore, and with greater accuracy. And in spite of all precautions they were sinking the Allies' merchant shipping at the rate of some half-million tons a month.

One of their headquarters was at Bruges—situated inland, but connected by canal with Zeebrugge and Ostend on the Belgian coast, the whole of which was now in the hands of Germany. The coast provided harbours from which German ships could make raids on the British coast as well as aeroplane attacks, which became a serious complication as war continued.

Thus, safe from attack themselves either by sea or land, German torpedo craft and submarines lay within safe base at Bruges, only sixty miles across the sea to the Straits of Dover. They were a constant source of anxiety to the "Dover Patrol," which for the last few years had nobly guarded the outlet by which the German submarines might escape into the Atlantic

The Dover Patrol and Zeebrugge

by the English Channel. The Patrol itself was made up of some eighty ships of every kind and description. Here were destroyers, steam-yachts, trawlers, obsolete battleships with short-range guns, mine-sweepers, drifters, fishing boats with crews from all parts of the country; there were men from inland towns as well as coast villages, merchants, artists, musicians, barbers, commercial travellers, who endured a life of danger and hardship during the years of war. The Patrol acted as "crossing-sweeper" to the hundreds and thousands of men who passed across the Channel between England and France, as well as to the thousands of merchant vessels which passed daily and hourly through the Straits.

But the German submarine commanders grew bolder and braver as time went on, and from their lair at Zeebrugge they would hurry out on the dark nights to attack the Channel ships.

For some time past a plan had been considered by which the homes of the submarine might be put out of action, and when, in 1918, Sir Roger Keyes became Commander of the Dover Patrol, he at once devised a daring plan for stopping the German raids at their fountainhead.

Briefly the idea was to block the end of the Bruges Canal at Zeebrugge, as well as the entrance to the harbour at Ostend—as hazardous an undertaking as ever fell to the British sailor. Every man concerned was a volunteer and fully aware of the danger he was facing—a picked man, who knew his job well, and could be relied on in emergency.

Now the harbour of Zeebrugge was as a sea-gate to the inland port of Bruges, its sandy roadstead guarded from the sea by a powerful crescent-shaped mole one and a half miles long, and connected with the shore by a viaduct built on steel pillars. Two heavy-timbered breakwaters, on each of which stood a lighthouse, led to the Canal. The harbour was known to be strongly fortified, machine-guns being stationed at various points to cover both mole and harbour.

It was truly a daring enterprise, for which a dark night, a calm sea, and entire secrecy must be combined.

An artificial fog or smoke-screen to hide the ships on their way was specially designed by Commander Brock of firework fame, who was unfortunately killed during the operations.

Three old cruisers—the Iphigenia, Intrepid, and Thetis—were filled with cement, and fuses placed so they could be sunk by explosion when in position. Motor-launches accompanied them to rescue their crews.

Then there were the twenty-year old cruiser *Vindictive*, with her false upper deck and gangways on the port side for the attack on the Mole, two old Liverpool ferry-boats, and other small craft. Twice the expedition actually started, but weather conditions failed, and twice they had to put back.

It was not till 22nd April 1918—the eve of St. George's Day—that the final start was made, and the strange little fleet set out for Zeebrugge. It was three hours before sunset, and Zeebrugge should be reached by midnight. From the destroyer Warwick, from which he commanded the operations, Sir Roger Keyes signalled the message, "St. George for England."

"Few who received that message expected to return unscathed, and in the block-ships—none."

It was a hazardous undertaking to approach a hostile coast teeming with enemy guns, without lights, ignorant of what new mines might have been laid, and at the mercy of the weather, a change in which might well expose the odd little fleet to the guns on the Flanders shore.

While the small craft were busy laying smoke-screens to

hide the destination of the ships, out at sea two monitors began a bombardment of the German coast defences with their big guns and seaplanes.

On went the little fleet on its perilous way, still hidden by the smoke-screen. The *Vindictive* was not far from the Mole, when a wind off the shore caused the fog to lift. The smoke-screen was rolled back—*Vindictive* and harbour stood clear to the foe. Up went the German search-lights, fixing themselves on the British ships, and German star-shells soared into the sky, while every enemy gun from mole and coast came into action. With men falling slain around them, marines and blue-jackets swarmed up the gangways of the *Vindictive*, and, under a withering fire, disabled defences and destroyed blockhouses. Suddenly a gigantic explosion rent the air—the viaduct had been exploded. A young English officer in charge of a submarine laden with explosives, with a crew of seven on deck, had steered her straight for the viaduct under heavy fire. Astounded and amazed at his audacity, Germans watched the little vessel, till she slipped between the steel pillars under the viaduct. Then the fuse was lit, the commander and his plucky crew jumped off into another boat and got away, while flames shot high into the air from the explosion. "There was no more gallant exploit in all that marvelous night."

The storming parties on the Mole were still fighting desperately, when the three block-ships steered straight for the Canal. The Intrepid, every gun firing, reached her destination, blew up, and settled down in the channel on the western side. The Iphigenia likewise swung into the channel on the other side, and sank.

Hardly was this accomplished than the signal sounded for the dash back to the *Vindictive*. All that was left of the storming party clambered aboard the battered ship, and, belching fire from every one of her broken funnels, she broke away. The German fire redoubled, and every angry battery did its worst, but she slowly made her way back to Dover to receive the Admiral's well-earned greeting, "Well done, *Vindictive!*"

It had been a wonderful night of brave naval exploits; and if it did not wholly succeed in its material objective, yet the moral result was splendid, and the work of the men who took part in the great adventure sent a breath of inspiration throughout the navy and a wave of patriotism throughout the country. They were indeed

> "Among the chosen few,
> Among the very brave, the very true."

31. THE CAPTURE OF JERUSALEM

"Go in and possess the land."

—DEUT. IV. 1.

The same year that saw the capture of Bagdad by General Maude and the retreat of the Turkish army, saw the occupation of Jerusalem by General Allenby and another great retreat of the Turks.

The capture of Jerusalem—the Holy City—was one of the great achievements of the war, but equally important was the long preparation that led to the conquest of all Palestine, and put an end to the 400 years of Turkish oppression.

One of the baits held out by Germany to induce Turkey to enter the war was that they should have complete supremacy in Egypt. The Turks were in possession of Palestine and part of Arabia. They now threatened the Suez Canal.

The boundary line between Egypt and Palestine in 1914 ran from Rafa on the Mediterranean to Akaba to the north of the Red Sea; therefore, to reach the Suez Canal, it was necessary to cross the desert land of Sinai. Dragging light pontoons, they made their way laboriously across the waterless sands in considerable strength, and on the night of 2nd February 1915 they tried to launch their craft and pontoons for crossing the canal. But British troops from Egypt were prepared, and a heavy fire quickly destroyed their light craft. True, four resolute Turks swam the canal, and landed under cover of darkness, but the next day the whole body of invading Turks were in full retreat across the desert, only saved from pursuit by a great sandstorm.

Another year passed before the Turks from Palestine renewed their activities in the desert of Sinai with designs on Egypt. They were fresh from their successful defence of Gallipoli, and, stiffened by German troops, they once more crossed the desert for a further attack on the canal. But they found awaiting them some of their old opponents of Gallipoli fame, Anzacs and others, and after two days of stubborn fighting, they were flying back on their camels across the desert, hotly pursued by mounted troops. Their losses were great in men, munitions and transport.

British preparations in Egypt now began for pushing them back once for all over their own frontier. From the shores of the canal a railway was constructed, and gradually pushed across the desert sands, while a water system was ingeniously devised by which pipes should carry the filtered water of the Nile for 200 miles right into Palestine.

Thus was fulfilled the old Arab prophecy that a deliverer should come from the West, and would enter Jerusalem on foot, but not until "the Nile flowed into Palestine."

Then a well-equipped Desert Column started off from Ismailia, and advanced with mounted troops and camel corps across the desert so quickly that the Turks retreated before them—even to El Arish—a seaport of some importance to the Allies, since there they could feed their troops by sea from Port Said.

Still on marched the Desert Column, some 2000 in number, in pursuit of the retreating Turks, until after a night march of twenty-five miles in the moonlight, they fought and captured a force of Turks, utterly surprised at their rapid movements. And early in January 1917, another moonlight march of thirty miles resulted in the capture of Rafa—the frontier city of Palestine.

And all the while, as they marched, the railway line followed, and the "waterpipes crept across the desert like a great snake behind the advancing troops."

The Turks had now withdrawn to Gaza, the "outpost of Africa, the gate of Asia," a city divided from the Mediterranean by two miles of sand-dunes. It had often been invaded through past ages, and no city in the world had been destroyed more often.

A British attack on Gaza in March 1917 failed, for the city had been very strongly fortified by the Turks, and a second attack three weeks later likewise failed, despite the help of some of the newly invented tanks from England, and the help of British ships which shelled the Turkish positions from the sea. But the enemy had received extra troops from their Allies, Germany and Austria, and the British failed to capture this stronghold.

In June 1917 General Allenby, who had already distinguished himself on the Western Front, was appointed Commander-in-Chief of the Egyptian Expeditionary Force, which was considerably strengthened by Territorials and Indian troops for the conquest of Palestine. The summer was spent in preparing for further advance. The Turks too were improving their lines. Their loss of Bagdad in March was a great blow to them, and they were determined to hold Gaza at all costs.

By October all was ready, and by a series of secret surprises, General Allenby captured both Beersheba and Gaza. While British and French warships bombarded Gaza from the sea, leading the enemy to suppose that an attack on Gaza would follow, British forces—mounted troops and camel corps—started off into the bright moon-light for Beersheba, some thousand feet above sea-level, among the hills of Judea. A sudden swoop was made on the city next day, and a rush of Australian mounted troops that evening captured 2000 Turkish prisoners and compelled a general retreat.

"A very strong position was taken with slight loss," General Allenby reported, "and the Turkish detachment at Beersheba almost completely put out of action." No time was to be lost. Gaza must be attacked now. On the night of 1st November Umbrella Hill, between Gaza and the sea, was stormed with startling suddenness, and soon the Turks were in full retreat along the coast.

Gaza had fallen at last.

"In fifteen days," wrote General Allenby, our force had advanced sixty miles on its right and about forty on its left. It had driven a Turkish army out of a position in which it had been en-trenched for six months, and had pursued it, giving battle whenever it attempted to stand. Over 9000 prisoners, 100 machine-guns and other stores have been captured."

The way was now clear for an attack on Jerusalem, the old capital of the Holy Land—sacred alike to Christian, Mohammedan, and Jew—which had been under Turkish rule since 1517.

On 7th December 1917 the British advance on Jerusalem began. The enemy had strengthened his positions with trenches and barbed-wire entanglements, while the summit of the ridge over-looking the Holy City was bristling with machine-guns. Rain was falling in torrents as the attacking forces advanced, the roads were heavy with mud, the hill slopes slippery and dangerous. A bitter wind was blowing, but in spite of difficulty and hardship, the troops advanced steadily, fighting their way. On the afternoon of 8th December command was given to London troops to charge the ridges above the city. Up the steep slopes the men clambered with a splendid courage, facing a very storm of machine-gun bullets. Many fell in the deadly struggle, but the survivors pressed on till the summit was reached, and a desperate bayonet fight took place. The Turks were no match for such hand to hand fighting. They broke and fled. Darkness found them in full retreat. Next morning the Turkish Governor surrendered, and on 11th December General Allenby advanced to take possession of the city. "Praise be to God that the British have come," exclaimed a Mohammedan from out the city. "Now we shall live in peace and prosperity. Our sufferings have reached an end."

Entering by the Jaffa Gate, the General walked on foot to the Citadel. There was no flying of flags, no bell-ringing or firing of salutes. The ceremony was utterly simple, utterly dignified.

Crowds lined the way picturesquely clad, Arabs, Syrians, Indians, and representatives of British troops. There was clapping of hands and strewing of flowers as the Conqueror of Jerusalem passed to read his proclamation to the "inhabitants of Jerusalem the Blessed."

"The defeat inflicted upon the Turks by the troops under my command," it ran, "has resulted in the occupation of your city by my forces. Since your city is regarded with affection by the adherents of three of the great religions of mankind, and its soil has been consecrated by the prayers and pilgrimages of multitudes of devout people for many centuries, therefore do I make known to you that every sacred building, monument, holy spot, shrine or place of prayer will be maintained and protected according to the existing customs and beliefs of those to whose faiths they are sacred."

Then he quietly left the Holy City.

And the whole world rejoiced that Turkish oppression of the great city so famous throughout the ages had ceased, and that Jerusalem had fallen into the hands of those who would give her freedom and justice.

32. THE CONQUEST OF PALESTINE

> "Through that great and terrible wilderness,
> wherein there was no water."

It was not till the summer of 1918 that General Allenby was able to complete the conquest of Palestine by a series of brilliant movements resulting in the capture of the Turks' last strongholds, Damascus and Aleppo. In the spring a large number of his best troops were called away to the Western Front to stem the great German offensive. It was therefore with an amazingly mixed army of Eastern rather than Western fighters that he began his new advance along the coast west of the river Jordan, "leaving the great Arab army under the Mohammedan, Prince Feisal, and a young Englishman, Colonel Lawrence, to march to Damascus by the desert railway route on the east of the Jordan.

The story of this Englishman, "who destroyed the thousand-year-old network of blood feuds, who built up the Arabian army, who planned the strategy of the desert campaign and led the Arabs into battle, who swept the Turks from a thousand miles of country between Mecca and Damascus" must be briefly told, for it is one of the most dramatic stories in the whole war.

A quiet visionary scholar from Oxford, an archaeologist in Mesopotamia and Arabia, this Englishman had learnt and loved Arab language and Arab history. Some time after the outbreak of war, he found himself a staff captain in Cairo doing work irksome to one of his mould. Applying for leave, he went across to Jiddah, the seaport of Mecca, on the coast of the Red Sea, to learn more of the Arab revolt known to be progressing against the Turks, who dominated the whole country from Mecca to Damascus. Now the strip of land known as the Hejaz, along the shores of the Red Sea from Mecca to Akaba, was held by one Hussein, an Arab chief in direct descent from Mohammed. His four sons had been living in the luxurious atmosphere of Constantinople; indeed, the third son, Prince Feisal, had for some years been private secretary to the Sultan, Abdul Hamid. On the outbreak of war, when Turkey had thrown in her lot with Germany, Hussein recalled his sons.

"Henceforth," he commanded, "thou art to make thy home under the canopy of Heaven that our house may not be disgraced."

Suiting the deed to his word, he sent them forth, each with a company of fighting Arabs, to patrol the pilgrim routes across the burning sands round about Mecca and Medina, in the province of the Hejaz. It was not till June 1916, after the important Turkish victory at Kut, that Hussein at last publicly denounced the Turks, and threw in his lot with the Allies. Then "with all the pent-up fury and hatred of 500 years of oppression and dishonour," the Arabs of the Hejaz rushed into the war!

The Turks, strengthened by Germans, at once attacked Mecca, the birthplace of Mohammed, the Holy City of Arabia, from her seaport of Jiddah. Within a month the Arabs had saved their city, taking over 1000 Turks and Germans prisoner. In all the fighting the sons of Hussein took a leading part, but Medina, where lay the tomb of Mohammed, still remained in Turkish hands.

At this critical moment Lawrence arrived from Cairo with Prince Feisal to help the Arab Army in its war against their common foe.

In him the Prince found a kindred spirit—an enlightened young man, modern in his views, enthusiastic in his work, and inspired with ideals. The Arab Prince and the young English staff captain agreed that the Arab rabble of fighters might be organised into a force to help in the work of freeing Arabia from Turkish control, and from that momentous meeting, Lawrence became the moving spirit in the Arab revolt. Persuaded by Feisal, he adopted Arab dress, and his knowledge of the language enabled him to go about the desert. Calling the headmen of the tribes together, he explained his mission, and over their camp fires he spoke to them of their past greatness and of their ability to drive away the Turks from their land, till in a high state of frenzy they promised their allegiance. For months on end he worked, until he had united most of the tribes of the Hejaz into an alliance of some 10,000 men. Then, marching along the waterless desert by the shores of the Red Sea, they attacked the ports on the coast till they reached the most important of all, Akaba, the last seaport in Turkish hands, once the naval base of King Solomon's Fleet, and strongly fortified.

The capture of Akaba involved a desert march of some 1000 miles along the coast of Hejaz in scorching summer heat, but Lawrence had laid his plans so well that the Turks were outwitted, and Akaba, not without some fierce fighting, was won with the loss of two Arabs only. But here a problem awaited solution. There were 700 Turkish prisoners to feed, in addition to the Arab army, numbering some 2500 Arabs, and they were forced to eat the "tough and sinewy camels which had carried them to victory."

Help was badly needed, and the morning after the battle, Lawrence started off to cross the Sinai desert, 150 miles of waterless sand, to Suez. It took him forty-nine hours, and this followed on the coast march of 1000 miles.

This all happened in 1917. In the summer, Lawrence met

General Allenby, and the powerful khaki-clad General, fresh from France, soon realised that this young Englishman, dressed as an Arab and fresh from Akaba, could be of immense use to him with his Arab army in the conquest of Northern Palestine.

From this time onward both Feisal and Lawrence were transferred from the command of Hussein, whose province of Hejaz had been wrested from the Turks, to that of General Allenby.

The Turks had learnt the value of Lawrence, and after Akaba they put a heavy price on his head, captured alive or dead.

While General Allenby and his army—Indians, Australians, and Yeomanry—marched between the river Jordan and the Mediterranean Sea toward Damascus, Feisal and Lawrence, with their army of Arabs freshly recruited from the tribes of the north Arabian desert, were to keep to the Turkish line of railway running from Mecca and Medina to Damascus on the far side of the river Jordan. A start was made from Akaba. The caravan consisted of 2000 baggage camels, 450 Arab regulars on racing camels, machine-guns, two aeroplanes and armoured cars, a total force of 1000 men mounted on camels, whilst others were added as they marched.

A march of 500 miles across uncharted desert had first to be faced and water carried, but this was accomplished in a fortnight, and the railway reached and telegraph-wires cut to prevent the Turks communicating with Damascus, Aleppo, or Constantinople when Allenby started his advance. About the middle of September Allenby began his move for Damascus, most of his fighting taking place on the Field of Armageddon—famous as the battle-ground of Israel and Judah. Nazareth, the headquarters of the German Commander, was captured on 20th September. At first the Turks had fought well to escape the net which was being cast round them, but now, pressed on all sides and "bombed into confusion" by British airmen from above, they began to surrender in large numbers. Meanwhile Lawrence and his Arab army played their part on the Turkish railway; they blew up Turkish trains, tore up rails, and dynamited bridges.

Then came the final round-up of the Turks and the brilliant dash to Damascus—"the most ancient of the world's cities." The Turkish armies had melted away under the joint charges of Allenby, a famous Desert Corps, and the Arabs. Enormous numbers of prisoners and guns had fallen into British hands, when early on the morning of 1st October Lawrence and his camel corps entered Damascus—a veritable dream city, its minarets and cupolas rising out of the early morning mist. All the inhabitants, together with "tens of thousands of Arabs from the fringes of the desert," crowded the "street that is called straight," as Lawrence, dressed in snowy white as a prince of Mecca, rode in on his camel with his picturesque bodyguard behind him.

A few days later, having established an Arab government in Damascus, Lawrence asked Allenby for leave to go home and, refusing all honours and decorations, disappeared from the land of his victories.

Meanwhile, Allenby was pushing now for Aleppo, whither all those Turks who had escaped destruction were fleeing. On 27th September his troops entered the city—the capital of Turkey-in-Asia. Turkish power was now completely destroyed and the way was open to Constantinople.

The loss of Aleppo was the last straw, and Turkey now sued for peace on terms of complete surrender.

It was only eleven days before the Armistice ended the great World War.

33. THE WESTERN FRONT—GERMANY'S LAST EFFORT

"This is the field where Death and Honour meet,
And all the lesser company are low."

—Herbert Asquith.

The beginning of the year 1918 found the position of the two opposing forces on the Western Front very different from that at the beginning of 1917. The Germans had been able to bring troops over from the East, owing to the dwindling away of the Russian armies, and for the first time since 1916 they were superior in number to the British and French. This superiority was not enough to give them actually a winning advantage, but they were able, owing to the exhaustion of the Allies, to concentrate their strength against chosen points, secure in the knowledge that the Allies would not be able to attack them elsewhere, at any rate early in the year.

The Allies needed reinforcements of fighting troops to turn the balance, but their resources in man-power were too depleted at the moment to furnish these. Germany knew this, and decided to risk all in one quick blow, which she hoped would prove decisive: her calculations were well made, but she failed to believe that the Americans would be able to bring into battle in time sufficient numbers to affect the result. There is no doubt that the presence of the Americans helped to turn the balance against the Germans. Ludendorff himself confesses "How many Americans had got across by April we did not know, but the rapidity with which they actually did arrive proved surprising."

The Germans also planned to use a new system of attack against the Allies, which consisted, briefly, in pouring in streams of men, who would keep coming on in increasing numbers, at those places where their first attack had been successful, thus going round and cutting off those places where the defence was particularly strong. In this way they kept their advance moving forward all the time, and saved numberless lives. The German defence against this method of attack was to have different positions stretching away back behind each other in depth, but the Allies as yet had not adopted this system. Thus Germany started the year with an advantage in numbers, and a new system of attack unsuspected by the Allies.

That an attack was coming was well known, and the Allied preparations for meeting it consisted in gathering together as large a force of mobile reserves as possible with which to counter-attack. These reserves were largely French troops, set free by the British extending their line down to the river Oise, an operation which naturally weakened the British reserves.

Although the mobile reserves which had been formed were naturally intended to help at any point on the Western Front which was seriously threatened, there was not yet, after three and a half years of war, one man in supreme control of affairs on the Western Front. The result was, not unnaturally, that the reserves were placed behind the French front in the Champagne country; and even when the British armies were in a position of the most extreme peril, there was a delay in sending help, owing to the fear of a German attack on the Champagne front. In spite of the most friendly working together of the British and French generals, and a common determination to defeat the enemy, it was impossible to expect the two armies to work together like a perfect machine, except when controlled by a single commander. In war, the time always comes when a decision has to be made quickly, and even a partially unsound decision is better than hesitation or delay. Lately, affairs on the Western Front had been controlled by an Allied War Council working at Versailles. This body of men, after discussion, came to a decision, and sent their orders to their respective generals. But there was bound to come a time when a decision was needed, and there was no time for discussion.

The Germans, therefore, had an additional advantage in that their campaign was organised and directed by one man, whilst the Allies had only a Council; and Ludendorff was not the man to miss taking advantage of this point in his favour. With all the Western Front at his disposal, he chose to make his blow against the British, who appeared to him to be the weaker of the two armies, bringing his main attack against the point where they joined, so as to cut off the British from the French and the common reserve.

Favoured by the weather, making most of his movements of concentration by night, and misleading the Allies by small distracting operations elsewhere, the German commander massed about 600,000 men on this front. His artillery power, greatly increased by guns withdrawn from and captured on the Rumanian, Russian, and Italian fronts, was stupendous, and, at the opening of the attack, there was one piece of artillery to every ten infantrymen.

The attack was launched against that portion of the British line which lay between the river Scarpe and the river Oise from Arras to La Fere, the point of heaviest attack being near St. Quentin. General Gough, with the British Fifth Army, was

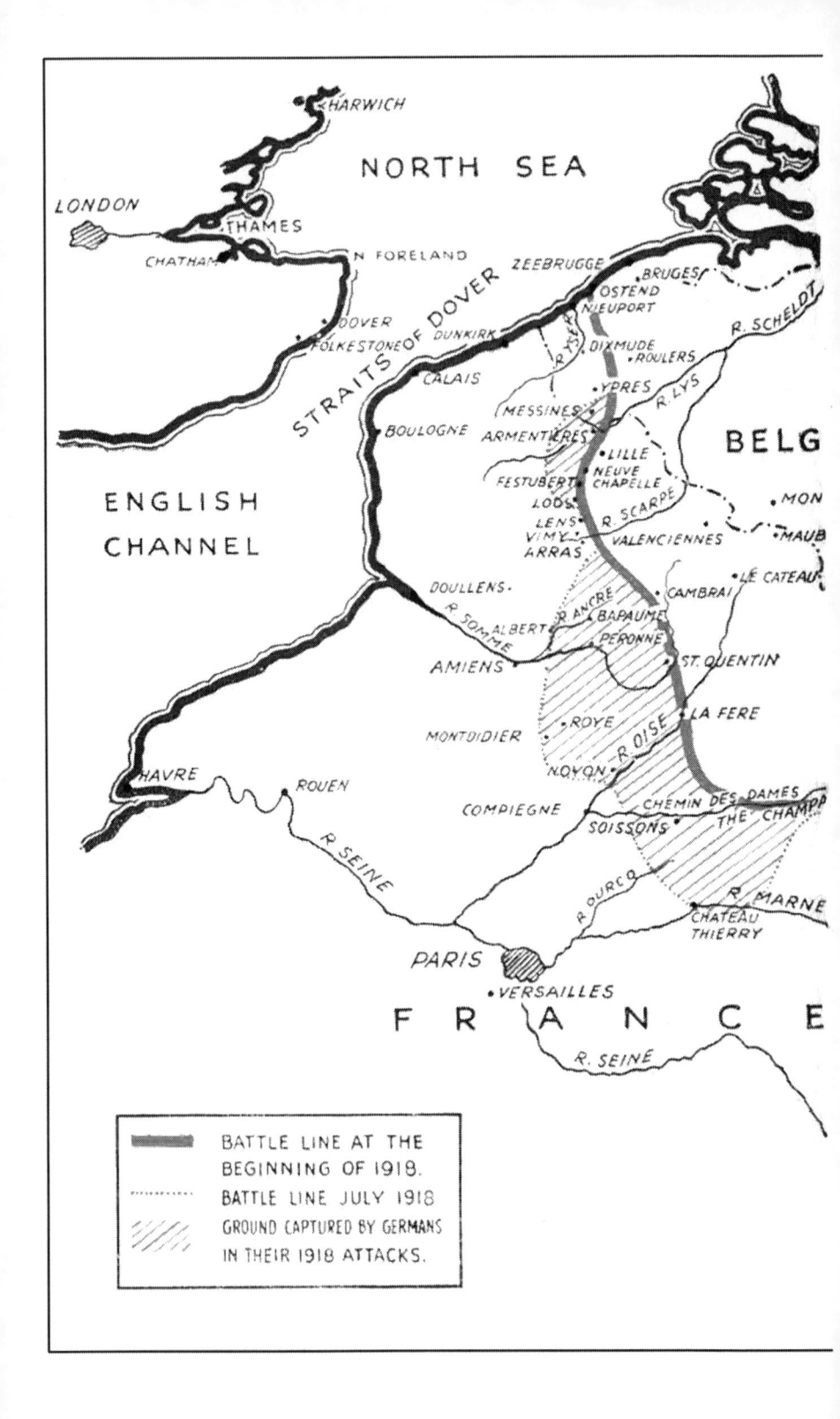

▬▬▬	BATTLE LINE AT THE BEGINNING OF 1918.
··········	BATTLE LINE JULY 1918
▨▨▨	GROUND CAPTURED BY GERMANS IN THEIR 1918 ATTACKS.

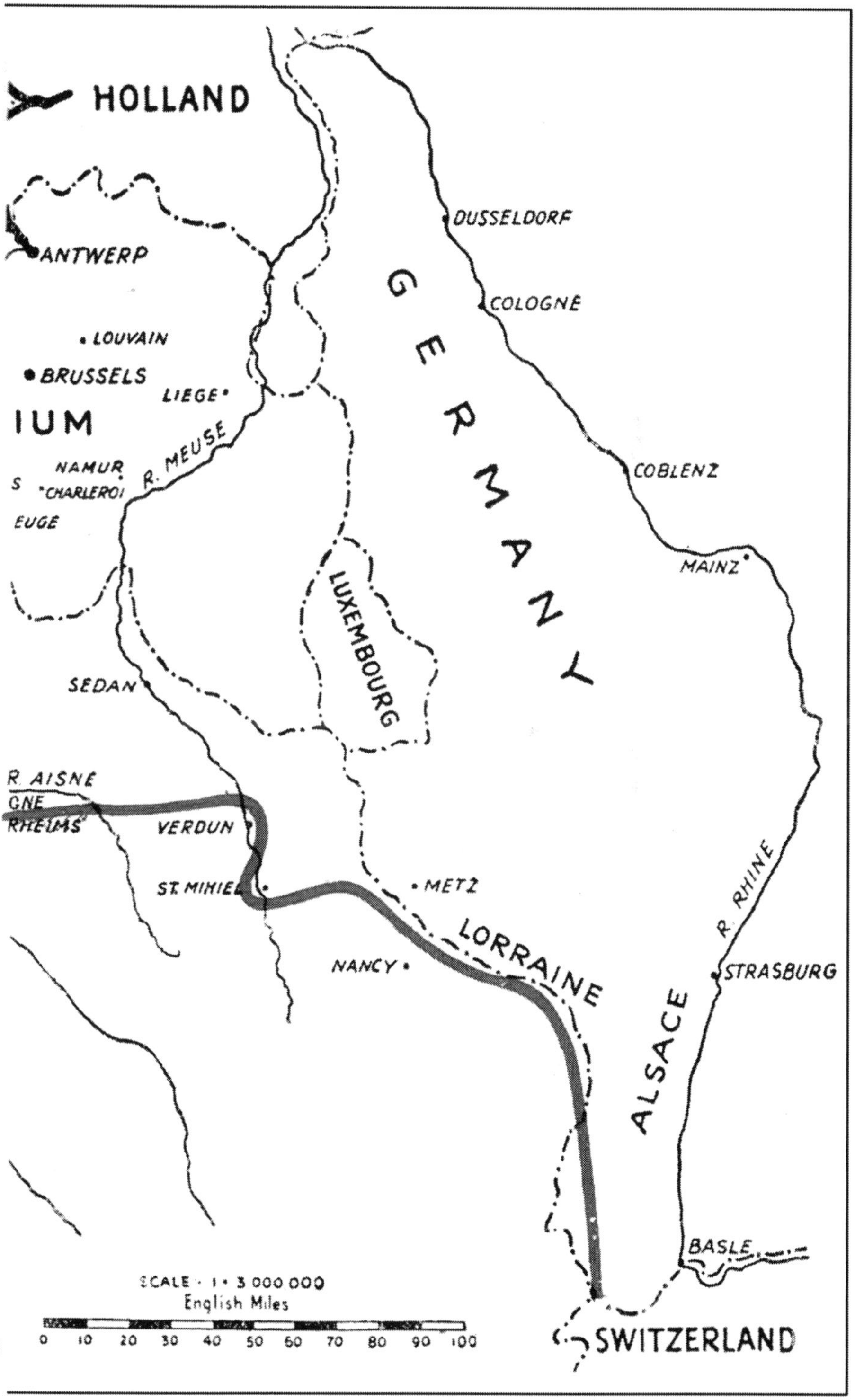

holding the latter portion of the line, with the Third Army, under General Byng, on his left, and the French on his right. In the early mists of the morning on 21st March, the great assault began. An hour and a half before day broke the colossal masses of German guns opened a bombardment of intense violence, penetrating in some places to a depth of twenty-eight miles behind the front line. Great use was made of gas-shells, and in the stagnant foggy air the gas, as it settled, clung to the ground. In the marshy ground below St. Quentin the mist and gas lingered longest, and it was here that the attack made its greatest success. The Fifth Army was, for the moment, broken; and in order not to lose touch with the Third Army on its left, it was forced to give up a great deal of the ground on its right. On 27th March, the Germans captured Albert, Roye, and Noyon, and in the first days of April were only nine miles away from Amiens.

The road to Amiens was barred firstly by a gallant body of men called "Carey's Force," commanded by General Carey, and composed of hastily collected engineers, cooks, labourers, signalers, grooms, mess attendants—any one who could hold a rifle, and then by the Australians and New Zealanders. In the meanwhile the gap between the British and French armies, made by the destruction of the right wing of the British Fifth Army, had widened, and there was grave danger of the two armies being separated altogether. The French mobile reserves were at last rushed up with extraordinary speed and efficiency, and the almost impossible task of repairing the defence was accomplished. The Germans claimed 90,000 prisoners and 1300 guns, and the Allied reserves had been used up.

The advance was, however, stopped for the moment, but the extreme seriousness of the situation roused the Allied Governments to the necessity of appointing one man to command all the forces on the Western Front. On 26th March Lord Milner, a man distinguished for his power of decision, hurried over to France and met M. Clemenceau at Doullens. In this little town, within sound of the rapidly advancing German guns, these men made the great decision. In spite of all the difficulties and delicate points involved, General Haig and General Pershing agreed unconditionally to serve under any one appointed, and General Foch was given the control of the allied armies: on 3rd April he was appointed actual Commander-in-Chief of all the allied forces on the Western Front. He at once set himself to the task of combining the strength of all these armies, but his task was rendered increasingly difficult by the fact that the Germans gave him no respite.

On 9th April they delivered another great attack between Armentieres and Lens, and after ten days' fighting had driven deep into the British line, and made it necessary once more to reinforce the defence with French troops. Fighting went on all the time, until on 27th May began the Third Battle of the Aisne.

This German attack was made between Soissons and Rheims, against a portion of the French defences, which they considered very strong, but against the new German methods of attack they gave way. The Germans surged over the Chemin des Dames, captured Soissons, and drove forward over thirty miles in four days to the Marne itself. British divisions were now brought to give help to the French; but before the enemy were stopped near Chateau-Thierry, they had taken 40,000 prisoners and 400 guns. On 9th June the Germans made yet another drive forward south of Montdidier and Noyon, extending their gains, and strengthening their line.

During this time the Germans had been bombarding Paris with a small group of guns, which were firing from a distance of nearly seventy-five miles. This was, of course, a range far longer than had ever been used before, and naturally no accurate results could be obtained, but the Germans hoped to strike terror into the hearts of the French people by means of these new and terrible weapons. The chief result of this unaimed and aimless fire was the destruction of a church on Good Friday, when many women and children were killed. The hearts of the French were only hardened, and amidst the great events which were happening on the Western Front, any other effect which this long range bombardment might have had was lost.

34. THE WESTERN FRONT— THE TURN OF THE TIDE

> "This battle fares like to the morning's war
> When dying clouds contend with growing light,
> What time the shepherd, blowing of the nails,
> Can neither call it perfect day or night.
> Now sways it this way, like a mighty sea
> Forced by the tide to combat with the wind:
> Now sways it that way, like the self-same sea
> Forced to retire by fury of the wind:
> Some time the flood prevails, and then the wind,
> Now one the better, then another best:
> Both tugging to be victors, breast to breast,
> Yet neither conqueror, nor conquered:
> So is the equal poise of this fell war."

At the end of June 1918, the situation looked very serious indeed for the Allies. The Germans had made great drives into the allied line, and the Western Front was more deeply bent and extended than it had ever been since it was formed in 1914. Still it was not broken, and there was yet hope. The fighting had become so intense and on such a large scale, with the enormous numbers of men and amount of material employed, that the war resembled the battle described by King Henry VI. in the words at the head of the chapter.

The Germans were still in a position to attack, the Allies were not; and Ludendorff, with his eyes on Paris, decided to make his next, and, as he hoped, his final effort, at the extreme point of the biggest bulge, where the line was naturally extended to its fullest extent, and therefore most likely to break. In order to keep the enormous masses of men, which he proposed to pour across the Marne, supplied with food and ammunition, he considered it necessary first of all to capture Rheims, so that he might use the railways running through that city. This accomplished, he was going to hurl his main forces at Chateau-Thierry, afterwards bringing in another attack from the north from the direction of Amiens.

Over-confident as a result of their previous successes, the Germans took fewer pains to conceal their intentions, and General Foch was ready for Ludendorff's opening moves. True he had very few reserves in hand, and these were by no means fresh troops, but in this case the attack did not come as a surprise, and the dauntless spirit of the French and Americans, coupled with their adaptability to the new tactics, enabled them to hold Rheims, and prevent a complete break through on the Chateau-Thierry front.

Ludendorff opened the battle on 15th July against General Gouraud's army in front of Rheims: he failed to gain the city. Meanwhile his attacks about Chateau-Thierry had partially succeeded, but on 18th July General Foch sprang his first surprise.

Despite the fact that the Germans still had a superiority of more than 250,000 men on the Western Front, he ordered an attack between Soissons and Chateau-Thierry. "We haven't the men," said the French Generals on the spot. "I know that," said Foch, "still you must attack the whole of the German Flank." Sheer courage and indomitable will won the day, and the Germans began to give ground. Soon they found them-selves congested and tied down in an ever-narrowing space, and to avoid annihilation, were forced once more to withdraw behind the Aisne. Foch was determined to press the enemy so long as he gave way before his blows, but to avoid a slow and costly struggle when the German resistance began to harden. When the Germans therefore were posted in strong positions behind the Aisne, he ordered an attack by the British on the Amiens front.

This attack was launched on 8th August, and met with immediate success. Montdidier and Noyon were retaken, and the attacks were extended north to the Scarpe. Albert was reoccupied, Peronne and Bapaume regained, and early in September all the gains made by the Germans earlier in the year had been eaten away. On 12th September the American Armies made an attack on the bulge in the line, at the point of which lay St. Mihiel, and gained a great success. They captured 16,000 prisoners and 443 guns, and straightened out the line at this point.

This operation completed the series of preliminary attacks, and General Foch was now ready for his knock-out blow. Paris and Amiens had been freed, he had gained sufficient ground for the free movement of his troops, and the German reserves were being rapidly used up. The Germans were now definitely on the defensive, but although they had given up hope of decisive victory, the Western Front was still unbroken, and they were in possession of large stretches of enemy territory.

Behind the battle line, at a distance of about forty-five miles opposite Cambrai, and of about twenty miles from the Argonne front, ran a line of railways through Metz, Sedan, Maubeuge, Mons, and Brussels. This was the spinal cord of the German armies, by which Ludendorff was enabled to move his reserves and stores from flank to flank. General Foch decided to strike at this spinal cord by means of two blows, one upon Sedan, and the other from between the Scarpe and the Oise through St. Quentin and Cambrai upon Maubeuge. On 26th September the Americans and French launched their attack in the Argonne, and on 27th September the British stormed forward in front of Cambrai. Both attacks met with immediate success despite the fact that Ludendorff had weakened his front elsewhere in order to stiffen his defence at these points, since he realised that if his lateral communication was cut at Sedan, the safety of all his armies would be seriously threatened.

As a result of this weakening of the front in Flanders, on 28th. September the Belgian Army, together with some British and French divisions, the whole under the command of King Albert, overwhelmed the thinly held German defences and swept forward with such vigour, that by 1st October they were in the outskirts of Roulers.

The whole line from Verdun to the sea was now moving forward, and the deadlock on the Western Front was broken at last. On 1st October the French captured St. Quentin; Lens and Armentieres were evacuated on 3rd October. Cambrai fell on 9th October, and Laon and La Fere were evacuated on the 14th. On 17th October the Allies were in Lille, and they had advanced along the Belgian coast beyond Ostend and Zeebrugge. The British alone had captured 36,500 prisoners and 380 guns. In the meanwhile Bulgaria had collapsed, and Germany, seeing the rapidly approaching danger of a general collapse, sent out her first request for an armistice on 4th October. This was refused, and Germany was informed that all invaded territory must be evacuated before a truce could be considered.

Ludendorff, however, was making a last effort to rally his forces, and his new plan was to fall back as slowly as possible, from one position to another, and he hoped to be able to keep the Allied armies out of Germany at least until the spring of 1919. The first stage of this retirement was a withdrawal to the line of the river Meuse, and a prolonged stand on that river when it was reached. In order to do this successfully it was necessary to hold the Americans in front of Sedan, and the British in front of Cambrai, while he withdrew his armies from other points, which were farther away from the line of the Meuse. The German troops had now pulled themselves together again, and Ludendorff's plan met with a certain measure of success, but just when he was endeavouring to assure the German Government that there was no cause for despair, news came of renewed successes by the British near Le Cateau and the Americans in front of Sedan. Ludendorff resigned on 26th October, and the next day, left General Headquarters.

On 31st October an armistice was signed with Turkey, which amounted almost to unconditional surrender, and an armistice, requested by Austria-Hungary on 29th October, was signed on 3rd November. Germany was now left alone, and the growing unrest in that country left no glimmer of hope in the minds of the Kaiser and his Government. Unmoved by these events, Foch was setting the stage for his next advance. On 1st November the French and Americans again drove forward, and on the evening of the 6th were in the southern outskirts of Sedan. Meanwhile the British armies were moving forward over the very ground on which the British Expeditionary Force of 1914 had first come into action. On 9th November, Maubeuge was taken by the British, whilst the 3rd Canadian Division actually entered Mons a few hours before the Armistice was signed.

At eleven o'clock on 11th November the Armistice was signed, the last shot fired, and the years of Armageddon ended. In Germany the Kaiser had abdicated, and there was revolution in the country. Although at this moment the military position of the German armies was hopeless for carrying on the war successfully, it is clear that the Armistice did not necessarily save them from complete defeat. They fought to the bitter end, and that end was brought about by the falling away of their Allies, and the revolt of the people at home against their military controllers. The fighting men on both sides throughout those four years fought grimly and magnificently for their respective countries, doing their duty and laying down their lives in silence.

> "Theirs not to reason why,
> Theirs but to do and die."

Amidst all the countless arguments of right and wrong, of victory and defeat, this one fact stands out as a reminder of the ennobling power of patriotism.

35. THE ARMISTICE

"No more to watch by night's eternal shore,
With England's chivalry at dawn to ride;
No more defeat, death, victory—O! no more,
A cause on earth for which we might have died."
—Sir Henry Newbolt (*Peace*).

The Great War was at an end. The guns were silent at last. The struggle in which 10,000,000 men had laid down their lives had suddenly ceased! The events of the last two months had made this possible. The plight of the Central Powers had been revealed to the world on 15th September, when the great Italian victory had left the Austrians powerless and hopeless. A cry of distress went to the American President pleading for a peace conference. But Wilson had already made known his famous Fourteen Points as a basis for any peace settlement, and he could not accept separate arrangements for Austria.

Ten days later the total collapse of Bulgaria and the abdication of King Ferdinand brought another request for an armistice.

The withdrawal of their one friend and ally in the Balkans made Turkey's surrender inevitable. General Allenby's victorious advance through Syria had played a leading part in the destruction of the Turkish armies.

Meanwhile the "Western Front" was reeling under the hammer-strokes of the Allies.

On 30th September, after the loss of the Hindenburg line, the Germans themselves saw that the war must end.

It was 1st October when Ludendorff sought an interview

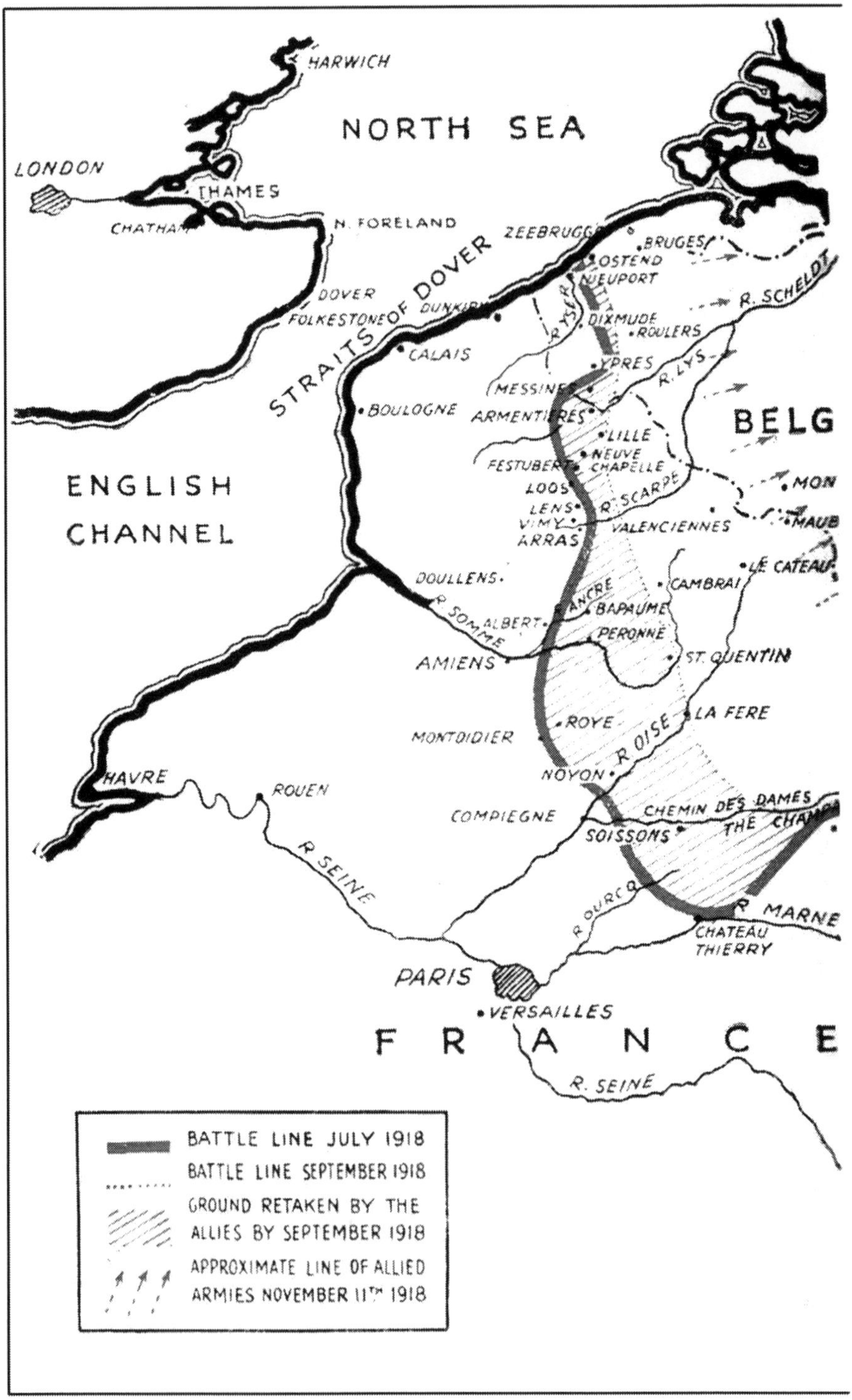

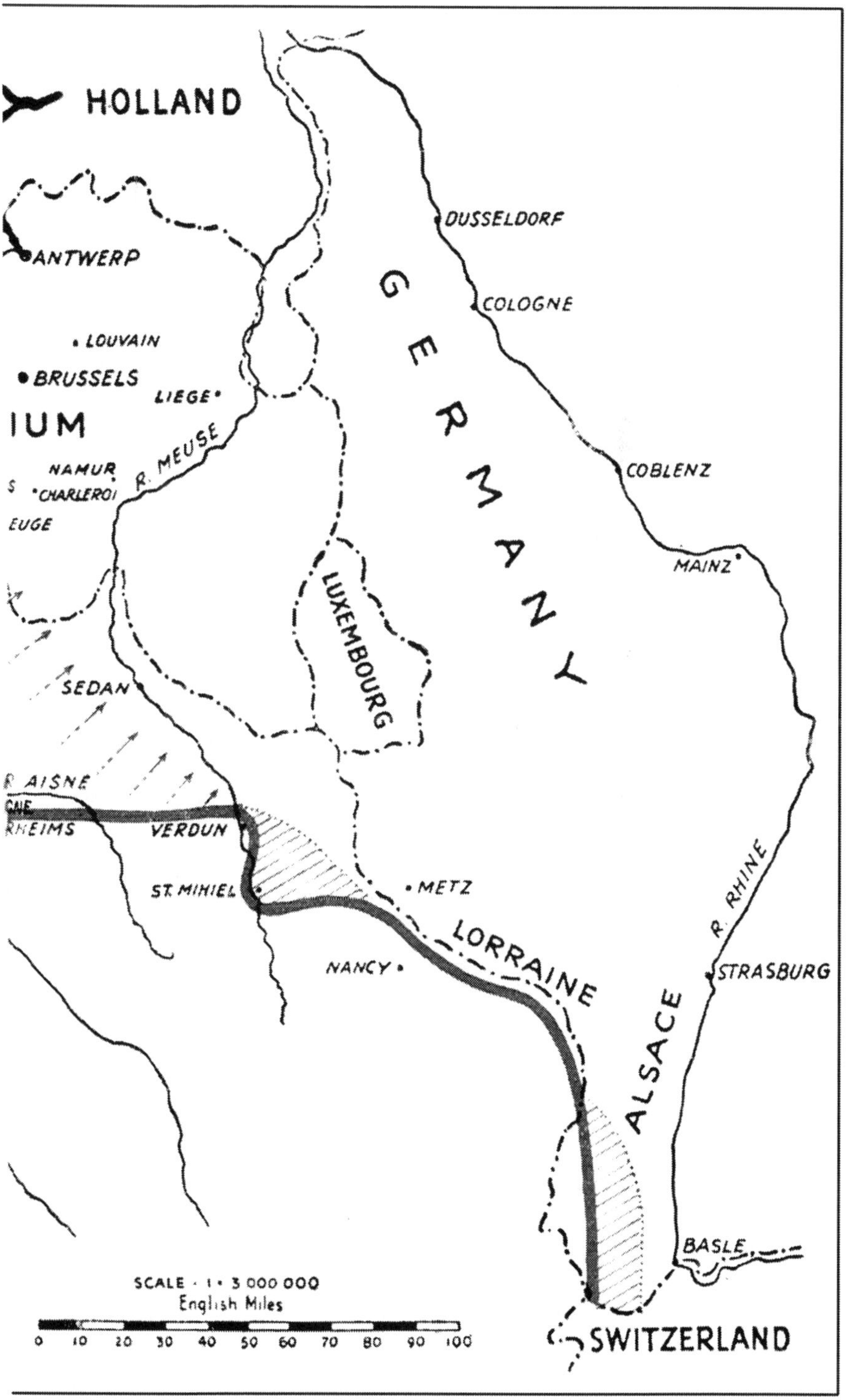
HOLLAND
ANTWERP
LOUVAIN
BRUSSELS
LIEGE
IUM
NAMUR
CHARLEROI
R. MEUSE
SEDAN
R. AISNE
RHEIMS
VERDUN
ST. MIHIEL
METZ
NANCY
DUSSELDORF
COLOGNE
GERMANY
COBLENZ
MAINZ
LUXEMBOURG
LORRAINE
ALSACE
R. RHINE
STRASBURG
BASLE
SWITZERLAND
SCALE · 1 : 3 000 000
English Miles
0 10 20 30 40 50 60 70 80 90 100

with the Kaiser. "Is not the new Government formed?" he had cried excitedly.

"I cannot work miracles," the Kaiser had replied.

"It must be formed at once," answered Ludendorff, "for the request for peace must go to-day."

A new Government had been formed under Prince Max of Baden, and a request to President Wilson to restore peace on the basis of the Fourteen Points had been sent.

"Throughout October the wires between Washington and Berlin were working at high pressure."

But so long as Ludendorff was in command, the Kaiser still on the throne, and the armies on the Western Front unbeaten, peace was impossible.

By the first week in November, Germany stood alone; Austria-Hungary, Turkey, Bulgaria had all surrendered. The end was not far off. The crisis was hastened by troubles from within. A mutiny broke out among the sailors of the Grand Fleet, who refused to obey their officers, and the red flag was hoisted on the great warships.

Workers' and Soldiers' Councils were formed, and a very tide of revolt swept over the land. Then came the cry, "Down with the Kaiser," and a cry for immediate peace. On the memorable 9th of November, Berlin workers and soldiers poured into the streets, and a Republic was proclaimed, and the abdication of the Kaiser was demanded.

"With a shivering hand" he signed the deed of abdication, and fled to Holland.

The once great German Empire had ceased to exist. Already the Germans had decided to request an immediate Armistice, and by means of wireless on the night of 6th November they asked General Foch how and where they might get through the line. A spot was selected, and at noon the following day a great blowing of bugles was sounded at the appointed place. The French stopped firing, and a German officer was seen, accompanied by a sergeant, "carrying an enormous white flag," and a bugler blowing loud blasts. He arranged for the reception of peace envoys, and returned. Towards evening the head-lights of motor-cars appeared, preceded by a gang of German navvies repairing the roads before them. The navvies were sent back, but the cars, each bearing a white flag, were admitted. The four officers and their attendants were then blindfolded, transferred to French cars, and taken by train to Compiegne. Next morning they were taken before Marshal Foch; the terms of the Armistice were read to them in his train in a siding in a wood, and they were given seventy-two hours to decide. All night long the Germans discussed the terms. They were severe, but they had no choice. Their armies were already in flight. At 5 o'clock on the morning of Monday, 11th November, the Armistice was signed, and by 11 o'clock the news had spread over the wide world.

The British Army had ended their fighting on the Western Front, where it had begun four and a half years before.

Everywhere the news was received with wild delight. The first impulse in London of the huge crowds that stopped work on the fateful day was to go to Buckingham Palace to cheer the King with enthusiastic and deafening cheers, which expressed their long pent-up feelings of joy.

Germany lay heavily burdened by her drastic terms of surrender. They included the immediate evacuation of all her conquered lands and a withdrawal behind the Rhine; the return of all the Allies' prisoners of war; the surrender of thousands of guns, engines, aeroplanes, submarines, and the main ships of the German Fleet.

The surrender of the Grand Fleet was not delayed. On 15th

November, the Rear-Admiral of the German Naval High Command crossed the North Sea in the cruiser Konigsberg to arrange with Admiral Beatty on the flagship *Queen Elizabeth* for the surrender of the Fleet. Escorted by a squadron of light cruisers, he entered the Firth of Forth, and steamed between the great ships of the British Grand Fleet to where the Queen Elizabeth lay at anchor. On board the great battleship conqueror and conquered made all arrangements for carrying out the terms of the Armistice.

A few days later the first contingent of German submarines was surrendered at Harwich. The scene was a solemn one. In the still dawn of the autumn, with the moon still lingering over the grey waters of the North Sea, one by one they stole out of the mist—their crews standing motionless on deck. Then each officer in charge formally handed up his papers and the design of the ship, and the British ensign was hoisted. It was a bitter humiliation, and one by one the commanders utterly broke down.

The following day the final and most impressive act of the naval drama took place in the Firth of Forth. It was an imposing sight as some 240 ships of the British High Seas Fleet put to sea soon after midnight to meet the great German battleships coming to the shores of Britain. There were five British battle squadrons of Dreadnoughts and super-Dreadnoughts, including Sir David Beatty's flagship the *Queen Elizabeth*; two squadrons of battle cruisers, bearing names already rendered famous—the *Lion, Tiger, Australia, New Zealand, Indomitable,* and *Inflexible*; six squadrons of light cruisers, and 160 destroyers. French and American ships were there too; all decks were cleared for action in case of trouble. Overhead flew airships and seaplanes.

It was 9:30 when the great moment arrived and the enemy Fleet hove in sight, and began to steam slowly between the two lines of the British Fleet. After four battle cruisers came nine large battleships, led by the Admiral's flag-ship, *Friedrich der Grosse*, followed by light cruisers and destroyers. It was noted that the sun suddenly burst out, and made a path of dazzling ripple between the two Fleets. Not a cheer rent the silent air as the procession of great ships made their way to the Firth of Forth, led by the *Queen Elizabeth*.

At noon the famous signal was hoisted from the flagship. "The German flag will be lowered at sunset, and will not be hoisted again without permission."

Then, and not till then, from every British battleship rose a very thunder of cheering, while Admiral Beatty stood on his bridge saluting.

At sunset the German ships lay at anchor, powerless in the grip of the conqueror. As a bugle rang out, the German ensign was lowered, never to be hoisted again.

The sequel must also be told.

The ships were interned at Scapa Flow in the Orkneys. There they remained till 21st June 1919. When it became known that a Treaty was about to be signed, and the German navy given over to the Allies, then the ships were sunk by their crews as they lay at anchor interned at Scapa Flow.

"It would have been painful for our good ships to come under the enemy flag, and this humiliating and painful sight is spared us by the brave deeds of our sailors in Scapa Flow. The sinking of the ships has proved that the spirit of the Fleet is not dead. It was done at my suggestion," added a German naval officer, "and I feel sure that in similar circumstances every English sailor would have done the same."

36. THE PEACE TREATY

"Then to our children there shall be no handing
Of fates so vain—of passions so abhorr'd,
But Peace—the Peace which passeth understanding,
Not in our time—but in their time, O Lord."

—R. E. VERNEDE.

The Armistice was signed on 11th November 1918. It was not till 18th January 1919 that the formal opening of the Peace Conference took place. It has been said that the time between these two dates contains more stirring episodes than years of battle.

Europe lay in ruins. The first days of wild joy were over. Kings had ridden back to their lost capitals in triumph—then they had visited Paris. The King of England and the Prince of Wales, who had played his part fearlessly in the Great War, had been followed by the King of Italy and later by King Albert of Belgium by aeroplane—all to be received with thunders of applause from the radiant, victorious French, in whose capital the Peace Conference was now to be held.

For weeks past, statesmen had been arriving from the four corners of the world to represent their countries. There were some seventy delegates in all—France, Italy, the United States, and Japan had each five, while the British Empire was represented by fourteen delegates. Thus with all their secretaries, an elaborate machinery was set up—but ultimate decisions were in the hands of first ten and then four men, M. Clemenceau, the French Premier, Mr. Wilson, President of the American Republic, Mr. Lloyd George, Prime Minister of England, and

Signor Orlando of Italy. When all were seated, on this fateful day, 18th January, President Poincare of the French Republic spoke.

"You will," he said to the great and varied array of delegates, "seek nothing but justice. If you are to remake the map of the world, it is in the name of the peoples and on condition that you shall faithfully interpret their thoughts and respect the right of nations. While thus introducing into the world as much harmony as possible, you will establish a general League of Nations, which will be a supreme guarantee against any fresh assaults upon the right of peoples."

M. Clemenceau was chosen President of the Conference. He—the "Tiger" of days gone by—was a born leader of men, and at the age of seventy-six was still full of his old vigour and activity. A patriot to the heart's core, he had fought for France in her last war with Germany, and signed the tragic protest against the taking of Alsace-Lorraine. He had watched Germany's preparation for this further invasion of his country. He knew that she was bent on crushing France, and that this struggle for world-dominion would be long and anxious. But even when things were at their worst, Clemenceau never lost confidence—his faith in France and her English ally never wavered. No other statesman had shown such courage in denouncing corruption and treachery in high places. When others despaired, this brave man hoped.

Three years of war had passed when a cry for M. Clemenceau rang through France. He was the one man who might save his country, in this her hour of danger. M. Poincare asked him to become Prime Minister. Only his duty to France resolved him to accept, and the old statesman shouldered the burden that younger men had declined. It had been a stirring scene when the Tiger of old days had delivered his first speech to the crowded house.

"Everything for France, everything for the triumph of right. Our simple duty is to stand by the soldiers, to live, suffer, and fight with them. The day will come when, from Paris to the smallest village of France, storms of cheers will welcome our victorious colours battered by shell-fire and drenched with blood and tears. It is for us to hasten the coming of that glorious day, which will fitly take its place beside so many others in our history."

His sincerity and patriotism raised the Assembly to the highest pitch of enthusiasm. The destinies of France were in the balance, and Clemenceau was the man at the helm. From the day he took office, his career was a series of triumphs. Through the dark days of 1918 he went almost daily to the Front, speaking with officers and men, cheering, encouraging, holding men firmly to their allotted tasks. When, in May, the German guns were thundering at the very gates of Amiens, and a strike of munition workers in and about Paris threatened the very existence of France, it was Clemenceau who persuaded the workers to go back to their tasks, himself maintaining an undaunted front. Had it not been due to Clemenceau too that the Allied command was united under Marshal Foch at the famous little conference of Doullens? Few had realised the gravity of the situation, but those who did, believed that Clemenceau—the Tiger—had saved the Allied cause.

This, then, was the man who was now placed in the supreme position of President of the Peace Conference.

Hardly second in importance was Woodrow Wilson, President of the United States. He had resolved to attend the Peace Conference in person, and fight for his Fourteen Points. On 4th December 1918 the George Washington, with the President on board, sailed from New York amid the wild shrieks of a thousand sirens, with aeroplanes flying overhead; and on 13th December steamed into Brest harbour through a double line of grey battleships and destroyers, to be greeted with a very thunder of applause. The following day President Wilson, driving through the streets of Paris, was wildly welcomed by a close-packed crowd—a public triumph indeed. Further triumphs awaited him in England and in Italy.

Men literally bowed down before him, and shed tears of joy in his presence. He stood for Peace and for Justice. He would lead them to the promised land, where wars were prohibited and blockades unknown. It has been said that the President had an opportunity vaster than had ever before been within the reach of man. It might have been a turning-point in the world's history. It failed for lack of moral courage.

Then came Lloyd George, the English Prime Minister, and M. Sonnino, Premier of Italy. The splendid services rendered to the British Empire by Lloyd George will never be forgotten. Through its darkest hours he steered the nation with confidence and with success. He had been a marked man before war broke out. His words in 1914 seemed to find an echo in men's hearts: "We have been living," he said, "in a sheltered valley; the stern hand of Fate has scourged us to an elevation whence we can see the great peaks of honour—Duty, Patriotism, Sacrifice. We shall descend again, but this generation will carry in their hearts the image of those great mountain peaks, whose foundations are not shaken, though Europe rock and sway in the convulsions of a great war."

The task before the Peace Conference was colossal. Nothing in the past could compare with it. For the first time in history whole nations had fought. 30,000,000 men had been wounded; nearly 10,000,000 had died. The great peace treaties of the past were child's play compared to this.

The map of Europe had to be remade. The forces of Right against Might had to be readjusted.

It was in a spirit of honest desire for a just and honourable peace that the delegates set to work.

The Treaty was studied, prepared, and discussed for six long months; 58 Commissions, holding over 1600 meetings, discussed by day and by night technical questions, and finally the Council of Four held 145 meetings. All men gave time, experience, and brains to the great work. No efforts were spared to obtain information, to get expert opinion from far-off lands, to extort the truth, the whole truth, and nothing but the truth.

A League of Nations was one of Wilson's Fourteen Points, and from the first he was determined that it should form part of the Peace Treaty. The idea was not new. The Hague Peace Conferences were not forgotten. Lord Robert Cecil had worked at the subject in England; Germany had issued a treatise on the same subject in 1918, while yet America was publicly announcing it. Through the winter months the complicated machines of Treaty-making worked laboriously. A rough draft of the League of Nations was finished on the very eve of the President's return to America on necessary business. The new Covenant provided for a Council of Nine Powers to meet annually and advise on any matters threatening to destroy peace. Members of the League were to agree not to make war without first submitting to the arbitration of the Council.

The President's return to America with this document, the first-fruit of the Peace Conference, in his pocket was bitterly disappointing. The country understood little of the difficulties of making peace. It did not approve of the President's long absence; it had no wish to be involved in European wars or European peace. His failure to command approval at home did not improve his position on his return to Paris a month later. The League was no longer the central interest. Its place was taken by the great question of reparations. How much should Germany be made to pay? The discussions were long and agitating. The Council of Four met twice a day, and talked with a deep desire to agree. Their conversation was at times "tragic in its grave simplicity." All the financial experts in the world could hardly name a sum that would be just to all. France had suffered the most, and demanded payment for her devastated areas, while America had suffered least.

But at last the Treaty was finished. It had taken six months to frame, The "Conditions of Peace" were contained in a bulky white book of over 200 pages written in both English and French. It was presented to the German representatives on the morning of 7th May, the 4th anniversary of the sinking of the *Lusitania*.

It was a day of brilliant sunshine. Within the great Hall there was deep anxiety. Would the Germans accept? When all the delegates were seated, the three Germans entered. The entire assembly rose to their feet and stood in complete silence while they took their places. The central figure was M. Clemenceau, sitting between President Wilson and Mr. Lloyd George. M. Clemenceau rose: "The time has come," he said, looking across at the Germans, "when we must settle our accounts. You have asked for peace. We are ready to give you peace. We present to you a book which contains our conditions."

The bulky volume was then placed before the German leader. He glanced at it, but let it lie untouched on the table. Without rising from his seat, he spoke slowly: "We have no illusion as to the extent of our defeat and the measure of our impotence. We know that the power of the German army is broken. We are not here to deny the responsibility of the men who directed the

War. We repeat that wrong was done to Belgium, and we are ready to make it good. In this Conference, where we stand alone, we are not without defence. You yourselves have given us an ally. The Allies have renounced a peace of force and inscribed a peace of justice on their banner. The principles of President Wilson are binding on you as well as on us. They require from us grave national and economic sacrifices, but the conscience of the world is behind them, and no nation will violate them without paying the penalty. I regard as the first task the reconstruction of the devastated districts. We have recognised the obligation and are resolved to fulfill it. The lofty conception of securing from the greatest tragedy of history the greatest advance, has been proclaimed and will be accomplished. Only when the doors of the League of Nations are open to all nations of goodwill can the goal be reached. Only then can it be said that the dead have not died in vain."

After a first rapid glance at the Treaty, the Germans wished to reject it at once, but they decided to take it home and make observations on it. This done, they returned on 29th May with a document denouncing the terms as impossibly harsh.

"We came to Versailles," they said, "expecting to receive a Treaty based on agreed foundations. We were indignant when we read the demands of the victors. Its demands are beyond the power of the German people."

The document was long and detailed. It "stiffened the back of Clemenceau and left President Wilson cold." A reply was presented to Germany on 16th June, the Allies had spoken their last word. The Germans must sign within four days or the Allies must "take the necessary steps to enforce the terms."

The Germans were distracted and angry. But the four days passed, and just two hours before the appointed time, a telegram of unconditional acceptance reached Versailles.

The closing scene took place on 28th June. The date was historic. It was the 5th anniversary of the assassination of Franz Josef at Serajevo. It took place in the same Hall of Mirrors at Versailles where, forty years before, Germany had dictated harsh peace terms to conquered France.

All the captured German guns which had filled the courtyard outside were removed. The streets were filled with French soldiers in sky-blue uniforms and steel helmets. Delegates of thirty nations were present.

As three o'clock sounded, a hush fell on the people and the two German delegates appeared. They were led to their seats opposite the table on which the book of the Treaty was placed. M. Clemenceau rose quickly and formally requested the Germans to sign. They rose, bowed, and signed their names. Then President Wilson, Mr. Lloyd George, M. Clemenceau and the other delegates signed. It was 4:30 before the ceremony ended, and guns outside began to boom. The delegates passed out into the open air, while crowds passed round the Four Men who had practically governed the world since the Armistice. At the place where the German Empire had been proclaimed after victory, it was now laid low after defeat.

Perhaps General Smuts expressed the mixed feelings produced by the Treaty when he said, "We have not yet achieved the real peace to which our peoples were looking. The work of making peace will only begin after a definite halt has been called to the destructive passions that have been devastating Europe for nearly five years. The promise of the new life, the victory for the great human ideals for which the peoples have shed their blood and their treasure without stint, are not written in this Treaty, and will not be written in Treaties. A new heart must be given, not only to our enemies, but to ourselves. A new spirit of generosity and humanity, born in the hearts of the peoples in this great hour of common suffering and sorrow, can alone heal the wounds inflicted on the body of Christendom."

37. A NEW EUROPE

"These things shall be! A loftier race
Then e'er the world has known shall rise,
With flame of Freedom in their souls
And light of Science in their eyes.

"Nation with Nation, land with land,
Unarmed shall live as comrades free,
In every heart and brain shall throb
The pulse of one Fraternity."
—JOHN ADDINGTON SYMONDS (*A Vista*).

All the old pre-war maps of Europe now became as "scraps of paper." By the terms of the Peace Treaty old boundaries disappeared, and new countries with strange names sprang into being; familiar landmarks were swallowed up; some provinces grew to double their former size; others shrank to a shadow of their former selves. Nothing but a close study of Europe in 1914 and Europe in 1919 can clear away the chaotic conditions which existed then, and indeed still exist to-day.

Kings and Emperors were in exile. Germany was a Republic; her ally, Austria-Hungary, was independent, both of one another and of those to whom they owed their ruin; Turkey in Europe practically existed no longer; Bulgaria's King Ferdinand had left his son, Boris, a shrunken kingdom, a reduced army, and a great war indemnity.

Such were the defeated nations. The Allies fared better. France had enlarged her boundaries by the return of her two lost provinces, Alsace and Lorraine, from Germany. What these meant to France, the whole world knew on that day, toward the end of November, when triumphant troops entered Strassburg, led by Marshal Foch. "The day of glory has arrived," he proclaimed to enthusiastic crowds. "After forty-eight years of separation, after fifty-one months of war, the sons of Great France, our brothers, are united once more. France comes to you as a mother to her dearest child, lost and found again. Vive la France! Vive l'armee! Vive la République!"

All through the long years when the provinces had been held by Germany, the Strassburg statue in Paris had been swathed in crape; this was now replaced by masses of flowers. The Allies were in possession, too, of the right bank of Germany's boundary—the Rhine. Belgians were in control of the northern section to Dusseldorf; British troops occupied the bridge-heads of Cologne and Bonn; the Americans were at Coblenz; and the southern part from Mainz to Basle was under France. Of Germany's eastern possessions, large slices went to Poland, including most of Posen and the corridor to the sea; East Prussia and Bohemia changed hands, and millions of Germans were transferred to alien rule. On her borders rose the new State of Czecho-Slovakia, with Prague as its capital. Austria had become the weakest of all the States of Central Europe, for large slices of her had already been annexed by the other large new State of the Jugo-Slavs— the greater Serbia of old King Peter's dreams, including Bosnia and Herzegovina and the once famous lands of King Nicholas's Montenegro. Rumania had been compensated for her sufferings on behalf of the Allies by great additions of territory, and, with Queen Marie, King Ferdinand at last returned to Bucharest to build the ruins of their fallen country.

Greece remained a kingdom for a few years after the Peace,

but after the final abdication and death in exile of King Constantine, a Republic was established.

Thus, freed from the domination of Russia and Germany, the Balkan States, with their history as old as Europe itself, were at last free to work out their own destinies.

Russia had no part in the Peace Treaty—she yet remained in the iron grip of Bolshevism. Thus was the face of Europe changed. "France was supreme on land and Great Britain on the seas." Familiar landmarks had been swept away. What would the future bring? The whole world yearned for peace. Would the League of Nations safeguard nations against future war?

President Wilson had sailed back to America as soon as the Peace Treaty was signed in Paris, only to discover that the idea of the League of Nations to which he had pinned his faith was not acceptable to his fellow-countrymen. The strain of the last months now made itself felt. Wilson was already a stricken man. He had failed, not because his ideals were not lofty and sincere, but because he had compromised those ideals. Now he could do no more. Sick in body, sick in mind, lonely and disappointed, he died in 1924. But the League, for which he had fought so hard, did not die. It stands for Universal Peace among the nations. The Hague Conference, too, stood for Universal Peace and the disarmament of nations. It belonged to an old world ruled by Romanoffs, Hohenzollerns, and Hapsburgs, who had made possible a World at War.

"Never again!" was the cry in every country of the men who had fought, the young manhood of the old world. Of these it had been said before the war broke out, that they were not as their fathers had been. They were seekers after money and luxury, even as were the sons of Hussein at Constantinople. The lofty ideals of past ages were gone. "The wheels of life were skidding on the greasy ways of wealth and ease."

War proved this untrue. The call came—a call demanding courage and endurance, for exposure, discomfort and weariness, for days and nights of cold and wet and misery—always in the presence of death, and gladly the youth of the world rose up and obeyed the call. The world had never seen the like before.

The spirit which inspired the war "when down the ancient highways your fathers passed to fight," must be applied to the attainment of peace.

A Peace Treaty—material and hard—changed the face of Europe. The League of Nations—part of that Treaty—was charged with a mission to end war.

"Never again!" was the resolute cry of those who fought in the Great War. But only a loftier conception of peace can make this possible. It's still a "long long way to Tipperary," the El Dorado of all our hopes, but the road thither has been made possible by a wondrous comradeship born in the War. Slowly, but surely, it was inspired by the great cause which united every fighting unit, by the spirit of sacrifice which bound them together.

> "We few, we happy few, we band of brothers,
> For he to-day that sheds his blood with me
> Shall be my brother."

This spirit of glad and happy comradeship of those "who went with songs to the battle" has survived the War. It is this very sacrament of brotherhood that must make the new peace.

EUROPE AFTER THE WAR
English Miles
0 100 200 300
ORKNEY IS
SCAPA
NO
(CHR
SCOTLAND
IRELAND
DUBLIN
NORTH SEA
JUTLAND
HELIGOLAND
WALES
ENGLAND
LONDON
DOVER
HOLLAND
ENGLISH CHANNEL
CALAIS
BELGIUM
BRUSSELS
G
PARIS
BAY OF BISCAY
FRANCE
BERNE
SWITZERLA
PORTUGAL
LISBON
MADRID
SPAIN
CORSICA
SARDINIA
BALEARIC IS
GIBRALTAR
MEDITERRANEAN SEA
MOROCCO
ALGERIA

RWAY
(ISTIANA)
OSLO
SWEDEN
FINLAND
(ST PETERSBURG)
PETROGRAD
STOCKHOLM
ESTHONIA
SEA
BALTIC
NMARK
COPENHAGEN
LATVIA
LITHUANIA
DANZIG
E. PRUSSIA
RUSSIA
BERLIN
WARSAW
ERMANY
POLAND
PRAGUE
CZECHO-SLOVAKIA
VIENNA
BUDAPEST
AUSTRIA
HUNGARY
RUMANIA
BLACK
SEA
YUGO-SLAVIA
BELGRADE
BUCHAREST
SERAJEVO
ADRIATIC
SEA
ITALY
SOFIA
BULGARIA
ALBANIA
GREECE
CONSTANTIN-OPLE
ROME
TURKEY
ATHENS
SICILY

Made in United States
Troutdale, OR
03/13/2025